The Illustrated Guide to
FINANCIAL INDEPENDENCE

LARRY FAULKNER

Illustrations by Douglas Brown

Published by

Faulkner Integrative Tactics (FIT)

This publication is designed to provide competent and reliable information regarding the subject matter covered. However, it is sold with the understanding that the author and publisher are not engaged in rendering legal, financial, or other professional advice. The mention of interest rates and other financial examples are merely that—examples. We provide no guarantee that your results would be the same as the illustrative examples contained in this text. Laws and practices often vary from state to state and country to country, and if legal or other expert assistance is required, the services of a professional should be sought. The author and publisher specifically disclaim any liability that is incurred from the use or application of the contents of this book.

ISBN: 9781671595262

Cover designed by Douglas Brown, albumartist.com
Interior designed by Danielle H. Acee, authorsassistant.com

To Lisa Faulkner,
who shares this crazy ride with me and
always believes that I can do it!

Table of Contents

1

The Point of it All...

"Only dead fishes go with the flow."
—Anonymous

FREEDOM! This is the reason for achieving financial independence! Can you imagine the freedom of being able to do almost anything you please today, tomorrow and the next day? Can you imagine this type of freedom each and every day for the rest of your life? I am referring to the life-altering ability to come and go as you wish, to live where and how you want, to travel to faraway lands if you like and to be able to finally do the things you only dream of doing as you toil away at work.

Financial independence gives you the ability to seek happiness and fulfillment on your own terms, without the pressures of a routine job to distract you. It also gives you a chance to develop your own unique talents, expanding your potential for happiness. This kind of freedom can give you almost unlimited options in life. The ability to obtain practically anything you want can be within your reach. The best part of achieving financial freedom is that you get to design a life that fits your personalized version of perfect.

Financial independence does not mean you have to stop working, although you certainly could. It allows you to choose what you will or will not do. You will have the option to work only when you want and only at jobs that satisfy you, challenge you or provide you with fulfillment.

Financial independence does not occur without knowledge, effort and perseverance! To have this kind of freedom, you must first become financially independent, and that independence can only be made possible by at least a moderate amount of wealth. This is the wealth you have the ability to create from scratch— starting from zero. I can show you the relatively easy to understand steps you need to take to turn your dreams for your life into a reality.

In this book, financial independence is defined as accumulating financial wealth to a point where you no longer require a traditional job to support yourself while living your chosen lifestyle. The phrase "chosen lifestyle" is a key descriptor in this definition that emphasizes the lifestyle that you desire. If you want a rich and famous lifestyle, it will require much more work up-front. If living an upper-middle-class lifestyle suits you just fine, it will require considerably less work.

My wife and I have put together a significant amount of wealth. A job is no longer a necessity to live the daily life we have selected and now enjoy. We both still work on occasion, but the difference is, we only do the things we want to do. We work at a job or task as long as it interests us or fulfills us. When a job or task is no longer worth our effort, or worth the pay and benefits we receive for it, we simply quit and move on. Most times we don't work at all. We are both firmly in the driver's seat of our lives.

Since becoming financially independent, we have traveled around the globe, which is our passion. We have been on an

African safari, traveled throughout China and traveled extensively in Western Europe. As I write this chapter, we are planning a trip to the Baltic Sea countries. Additionally, we have traveled extensively throughout the United States, visiting almost every state in the union, including most of the Hawaiian Islands and Alaska. It is not unusual for our trips to be a month long. We can come and go as we wish, stay as long as we want and we only do things that are important to us. This is our ideal life, but I understand that may not be your ideal life. The beauty is, you get to choose.

My wife and I did not accumulate our wealth by making huge salaries. We were never near the top-earning tiers; we were simply middle-class workers. She is a previous ER nurse, paramedic and firefighter, and I am a retired cop. We did those jobs while raising three children in a blended family and surviving prior divorces that significantly impacted our financial status. We did not come from wealthy families. We were not loaned or given large sums of money from our parents. Our wealth was built from the ground up from almost nothing. We started with minimal financial resources and created financial independence while supporting a family of five.

The fact that we built our wealth from scratch is an important point because it blows up the preconceived notions people have when it comes to achieving their own dreams. For example, I have heard many nurses and cops say things like, "You can't create wealth on a middle class salary." Placing those kind of limitations on yourself is entirely the wrong way to think about building wealth. Your attitude about wealth-building is hugely important to your financial success (see Chapter 2).

The Millionaire Outlook Study (2012) by Fidelity proves that my wife and I are not all that unusual. Most millionaires are self-made. Roughly 86 percent created their own wealth from scratch[1], just like we did. The latest Credit Suisse Research Institute's Global Wealth Report also shows that millionaire households were on the rise in 2017 and 2018. Roughly one in 20 people are now millionaires[2]. In other words, plenty of regular people are figuring out how to achieve their own version of financial independence!

This book focuses on the important stair steps leading to financial independence—not retirement. This is not a "retire early" book! You can be significantly well-off long before you retire. As you ascend each step on the stairs to wealth, each step makes the next step possible. None of these steps are unworkable. None of the steps fall outside the mainstream concepts of good personal financial practices or good portfolio management (management of your investments).

The information in this book creates a system. All the steps work together. The system is quite powerful when it is utilized. It is so powerful it can turn a middle-class person into a reasonably wealthy person. Rich people who utilize it get richer. Rich people who don't utilize it become poorer and sometimes just go broke.

The goal of this book is to explain this personal finance system and the accompanying investing concepts in a simple, straightforward manner without boring you. All the chapters in this book are short and concise. Each chapter is summarized at the end with illustrations to engage the various learning types in our population. Once you cut through all the extraneous information, as we have done here in this concise guide, you'll find it's not that complicated. Still, to build wealth, you must understand certain basic financial principles and how they fit together or you will waste your precious time and valuable financial resources.

Many people have a vested interest in charging you a lot of money to perform many of these wealth-building steps for you.

They have a significant financial interest in making it seem as complicated as they possibly can. It is not complicated once you break it down. If it were, my wife and I could not have successfully achieved our goals. We achieved all of our written goals. In fact, we crushed those goals and exceeded our initial expectations despite several setbacks!

Your entire journey starts with a simple, ironclad rule. You are in charge of your own life. You and you alone are responsible for the vast majority of outcomes and consequences you experience in life. That fact is hard for many people to accept, but it is as true as anything you will ever know. Once you understand the ironclad rule of accountability, building wealth becomes much easier.

If you want to become a millionaire and are willing to commit time and energy to this goal, then you can become one. It is as simple as that. I can show you how to do it! Plenty of people have done it before you and you can certainly do it as well. Trust me, it's not that hard for committed individuals or a family to achieve their own version of financial independence.

There are really only two choices. You can choose freedom and get control of your approaching future or you can procrastinate and go with the flow until your options become limited—usually severely limited. If you are not in life's driver seat, then other people control what you will or will not do each and every day of your life. The more money you are able to access outside of a job to meet your daily living needs, the more control you regain over your destiny.

If you love your job and home life, then you are probably not feeling any discomfort in the level of control you have over your everyday life. If you are only lukewarm about your job or you absolutely detest it, you are definitely feeling a loss of control and a drop in your overall life satisfaction. Even if you love your job today, events could occur tomorrow (like getting a new supervisor) that will completely change your work situation and your attitude.

Money buys options! Financial independence gives you the ability to exert control over what you will or will not do. In turn, increased control over your life will likely be followed by an increased sense of contentment. In other words, money creates the conditions that give you the best opportunity for finding your version of happiness and life satisfaction. Take control and begin your journey to create your own version of an ideal life made possible by the power of financial independence! You can ascend your own stair steps to wealth.

 FINANCIAL INDEPENDENCE

NO LONGER REQUIRE A

TO SUPPORT YOU

 FINANCIAL INDEPENDENCE

2

The Stair Steps to Wealth

"The number-one reason people fail in life is because they
listen to their friends, family, and neighbors."
—Napoleon Hill

Do you want to build significant, life-changing wealth while
being a regular working stiff? We did, and many people we
know accomplished this goal as well. This book explains the system of creating financial independence for the average employed
person who is earning a weekly or bi-weekly wage.

Some of my co-workers already knew how to build wealth
when they first started their police careers. Those people achieved
far better results than we did because they already had the knowledge and skills necessary to succeed in achieving their financial goals.
Unfortunately, my wife and I had to learn as we went, and that
wasted precious time, money and resources. Our efforts still left us
financially independent and secure with one million plus in various
financial assets and several constantly flowing income streams.

Financial independence is most easily achieved by creating
multiple, diverse income streams. An income stream is a regular

inflow of capital (money) from a source you have previously set up or created. The more income streams you build to fund your life, the more freedom you create within your life. The more independent your income streams are from one another, the more secure your financial life becomes.

Here are just a few examples of income streams:

- Income from your regular job
- Income from a side hustle (side job)
- Income from your investment portfolio
- Income from a pension
- Income from disability payments
- Income from a business you created
- Income from your hobbies
- Income from rental properties
- Income from social security
- Income from military service or military reserves
- Income from additional sources

If you have a significant other, he or she should also go about creating multiple income streams. Income streams are vital to financial independence.

In the old days, people worked for one company their entire lives. When they retired, the company took care of them with a pension. Few people now have an opportunity for a pension. With the exception of government service and a few other jobs, pensions are almost extinct and will remain so. Today's workers are similar to independent contractors, going from employer to employer. That makes the information in this book even more vital for your financial success and well-being. You have to build your own financial empire and you can expect little (legitimate) outside help to do it.

In addition to our financial assets, between the two of us, my wife and I have developed a half-dozen income streams for our use. Some of these income streams require effort on our part to maintain, but others require little to no maintenance. Income streams that require minimal effort to maintain are called passive income streams. Passive income streams are very cool because they don't require a great deal of your time once they are set up and running. Of course, no one gives you these income streams. You have to go out and create them. That requires knowledge, work, perseverance and determination.

One of the most important passive income streams you can create is an investment portfolio because the flow of money from it is totally under your control and it can become quite large. As a passive income stream, it takes very little effort to maintain it.

An investment portfolio is a large pile of invested money that you create. The funds are held in multiple, diverse investments. When all the investments are considered as a whole, like parts of a pie, the group of investments is called an investment portfolio. Diverse investments are safer and more resilient than a large investment in any single asset (an investment or something else of value). You spread the risk of losing money over many investments that reflect different assets classes or parts of the financial markets. This approach has been proven over the years to be much safer and more profitable than having any single investment—including real estate.

When you stop working, or whenever you choose, the portfolio generates passive income that can flow into your bank account for your use. Once it is set up, it will require minimal time and effort on your part to maintain—as opposed to working at your job or in your business.

There are literally thousands of ways to create wealth. Creating a large investment portfolio is only one. I know people who have become wealthy by starting their own businesses or by building a real estate empire from scratch. These people become experts in those areas and know how to build wealth using their own customized paths.

None of the wealthy people I know, and I know quite a few of them now, became a success overnight. They all put in time and effort and suffered through initial losses to earn their current consistent wins. They all worked very hard and earned their right to be financially independent. No one gave it to them, and it didn't come easily—especially at first.

There are plenty of books and vast online resources dedicated to the subject of creating great business and real estate empires. This book is different. This book is about creating financial independence in your life (meaning that you no longer require any particular job to make a living) by creating a large and diverse investment portfolio that will generate significant income for your use in the future.

The earlier you begin saving and investing your wages, the easier it becomes to harness the power of money, time and compounding interest to create a significant income stream. If you didn't start early, don't worry. You can still accomplish your financial goals. A quick search on Google will reveal that people have become quite wealthy as seniors. You will just have to overcome more obstacles to create wealth.

I have been involved in teaching basic and advanced personal finance concepts to various groups, both during and after my law enforcement career. I am a Certified Financial Education Instructor with significant experience teaching financial principles. The stair step system of wealth creation has been repeatedly proven to work for the average working person. The steps contained in this concept integrate all basic household financial skills and personal wealth-building techniques into an easy, comprehensive structure. The value of the stair step concept is that it clearly shows that the successful implementation of any single step is highly dependent upon the previous step being completed correctly.

The stair steps represent a conceptual framework that allows your mind to organize, file and then apply wealth-building information to your investment portfolio to generate an income stream. Without a comprehensive understanding of how everything works together, you are stuck trying to absorb a bunch of disconnected, seemingly disparate nuggets of information. Absorbing information in this manner makes it much harder to apply personal financial skills and techniques to their maximum effectiveness. The stair steps also assume you are starting from zero money saved. Here are the steps:

1. Financial goal-setting
2. Create income(s) from your job(s) and/or businesses.
3. Budgeting your income
4. Saving your money
5. Investing your savings regularly and over time

Following these steps will allow you to create an investment portfolio that will help support your financial independence.

Based on our experience, we strongly recommend your investment portfolio be at $1,000,000 or more. It may sound like a lot of money, but it is actually very achievable for a middle-class, working couple or a single person. This is not an arbitrary number. Very smart people have already determined that you can remove approximately four to five percent annually from your $1,000,000 portfolio and your stockpile will be preserved and even continue to grow. Assuming you have at least $1,000,000, your portfolio will provide you a minimum of $40,000 annually (on average) in addition to the other income streams you have already built. As your portfolio grows in size, it will create even more income. Essentially, your income stream from your investments becomes sustainable and renewable. As you age, four percent of a larger investment portfolio generates larger annual payments. You can soon remove around $50,000 annually, then $60,000 and so on, without damaging your income-generating machine.

YOU DON'T HAVE TO WAIT UNTIL YOU RETIRE TO HAVE FINANCIAL INDEPENDENCE

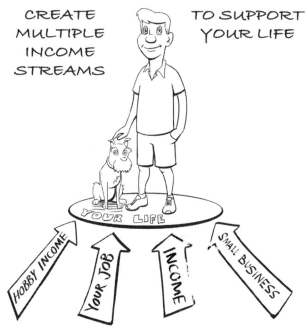

CREATE MULTIPLE INCOME STREAMS

TO SUPPORT YOUR LIFE

YOUR LIFE

HOBBY INCOME

YOUR JOB

INCOME

SMALL BUSINESS

STAIR-STEP METHOD OF WEALTH CREATION

WEALTH MACHINE

INVESTING

SAVINGS

BUDGET

INCOME CREATION

GOAL SETTING

NO MONEY

THESE STEPS CREATE A WEALTH MACHINE!

3

Goal-Setting

"Successful people do what unsuccessful people are not willing
to do. Don't wish it were easier; wish you were better."

—Jim Rohn

You can build wealth and achieve financial independence—but only if you are willing to do things differently than your peers. This book will show you how living a different type of lifestyle will be more rewarding and allow you to become an elite, high financial achiever. I will show you not only how to achieve financial success, but how to meet and exceed your goal of creating financial independence in your life. The path is a little more difficult in the beginning, but so much easier and incredibly rewarding only a short time later.

You become financially independent the same way you accomplish anything worth doing: by goal-setting and then working toward goal achievement. Here are the steps involved in goal-setting for wealth creation:

1. Evaluate where you stand today.
2. Create and then write your goals.
3. Research your goals.
4. Create an action plan to reach your goals.
5. Set a timeline for obtaining each goals.

Create and set goals that get you excited, like getting out of debt, becoming a millionaire and becoming financially independent. Most people only set career goals and stop. A high achiever sets financial goals, personal goals and even relationship goals (see my book, *Messages From Your Future: The Seven Rules for Financial, Personal and Professional Success[1]*). Achieving most big goals will require sustained effort on your part. You must emotionally connect with each of your goals in order to create enthusiasm to work toward them. Your enthusiasm, in turn, will help keep you motivated to do what is necessary to succeed.

The first step in achieving financial independence is evaluating where you stand financially at this exact moment in time. Create a list of your total assets (things of value) such as your bank accounts, cash and other assets (physical items you own of significant value). Then subtract the debt you have accumulated, including credit card debt, personal loans, car loan, mortgage, school loan debt and miscellaneous debt. This will give you your net worth. Hopefully you have a positive net worth rather than a negative one. Unfortunately, most people suffer with a negative net worth. However, even with a negative net worth at this moment in time, you can still achieve your goals.

Achieving your financial goals is centered almost entirely on the knowledge and strategies you employ. Financial goals generally require research to understand how you can achieve them. With financial goals in particular, this step is critical. Technical knowledge is required to build wealth. Don't panic! Technical does not mean difficult. If you have an incorrect understanding of how your goals will be obtained, however, you will waste a lot of time, money and energy.

Create a written plan that includes not only your goals but also lists multiple sub-goals or benchmarks that you must achieve on your journey. Sub-goals allow you to mark and celebrate your progress. Celebrating success is vital (not an afterthought) and gives you a feeling of accomplishment and purpose as you continue to move forward over time. Meeting benchmarks will also help motivate you to reach the next sub-goal, and the next and so on, until you achieve your major goal(s). All goals must include a realistic time frame for achievement (write the date next to each of your goals). Without time frames for action and achievement, it's just a wish or daydream.

Once you have your written goals with appropriate time frames, write down the necessary steps (that you've discovered through research) to achieve all stated sub-goals and goals. Then, take forceful action to advance your written plan and achieve your goals on schedule to the best of your ability. If you achieve your goals a little later than planned, that's okay. The accomplishments and benefits are still real and tangible.

Writing down your goals has power in our universe and is the important first step in creating the future that you want, rather than stumbling into the future by failing to plan. Do not skip this step! Writing down a goal gives your non-material thoughts a physical presence in this world. This is the first step in creating the inertia needed to push you forward to the finish line. I usually tape my written goals to my bathroom mirror. I recommend that you do the same. There is no escaping them when you do that! You look at your goals as you get ready to take on each day, which helps you focus on what your day is really all about.

Successful people and the self-made rich are relentlessly goal-oriented. They become excited about goal achievement because they have made this process work for them so many times in the past. Money is important to them because it is the primary tool they will use to create a life of freedom. The rich make no apologies to anyone for accumulating wealth in legal and ethical ways.

The self-made rich also think long-term (strategically) and have the ability to resist the instant gratification of buying things they don't actually need. Work on thinking strategically in all aspects of your life, and particularly in your financial life.

We all have problems that could easily derail our progress, just as we all have our own amazing talents that can help us succeed. I have personally overcome many deficits that could have derailed not only my finances but my life as well. For example: I had a challenging childhood; I still struggle with adult attention deficit disorder; I suffered through two previous divorces; and I have struggled in the past with post-traumatic stress due to physical and emotional trauma related to my law enforcement career.

I also face challenges in the physical act of writing. Every day, I must overcome an old work-related injury to my neck and shoulders that initially prevented me from typing this manuscript (my second book). I overcame all of these difficulties by using goal-setting and seeking help for medical and/or psychological issues promptly when they blocked progress toward my goals or interfered with me living the life I have decided to live. Seeking assistance promptly minimizes your struggles with physical and mental issues that can derail you. It also minimizes the amount of time it takes you to get past the issues that are holding back your progress.

As I said, we all have talents. My talents include knowing the power of goal-setting. My ability to think strategically has saved me from many terrible situations. I enjoy writing and teaching, I am good with people and my personality is a mix of creative and analytical. My lovely wife is the opposite. She thinks analytically first and creatively to a lesser extent. Our natural abilities complement each other nicely and we're a terrific team.

Do you think you have challenges that hold you back in life? Ex-convicts who have gone straight, elderly citizens, the disabled and even addicts in recovery have become millionaires by ignoring their limitations and maximizing their talents. All of these folks obtained wealth by setting goals, persisting in the face of significant obstacles, having a strong work ethic and doing things differently than their peers. They also made many mistakes along the way, but rather than letting the mistakes derail them, they learned from their errors, kept a positive attitude and moved relentlessly forward. You can as well!

People who succeed push past their serious limitations every day to achieve their goals. They also overcome the problems they encounter that block their forward progress. No one ever escapes issues and complications on their way to goal achievement. The successful accomplish their goals in spite of the inevitable roadblocks.

The relatively new field of positive psychology has studies and data to prove that your attitude about your roadblocks are hugely important. If you see your roadblocks as a sign of inevitable failure, experience rising anger, succumb to fear or personal shame then you can't overcome the problems that are inevitable[2].

The most important tip that will help you accomplish your goals is to stay positive. Keeping a positive attitude is really a matter of focus. If you focus on what holds you back, all you see are problems and roadblocks. If you focus on your goals, you begin to see the opportunities and strategies that are right in front of you. Not because I say this is the correct strategy, but because the data says it. In fact, the data implies that one of your goals should be to maintain a positive attitude in the face of inevitable problems[3].

Positive thinking isn't meant as some type of Pollyanna magic in this context. You will suffer setbacks and even outright failures. This is a fact and it is very normal. Use those failures to motivate you. Without a positive attitude, you will be unable to overcome obstacles and push through life's disappointments and progress toward your stated goals. Pessimism never helped anyone accomplish any significant goal! Your attitude is always an important component of wealth creation.

Thinking has real power in our physical universe. Here is a trick I use to keep myself positive: I go out of my way to encourage and help others achieve their goals. Helping and encouraging others helps keep you in a positive frame of mind. It also allows you to make many friends and connections along your journey to create the future you are working so hard to obtain. After all, we all need cheerleaders in our lives!

Written goals are a physical manifestation of your thoughts and dreams. You can bend the course of universal events to your will—in reference to your own actions and outcomes stemming from those actions. The trick is to focus your energy and attention on the steps necessary to achieve your goals. You are much more capable than you think. In life, most of your limitations are actually self-imposed and don't really exist, except in your mind and in your emotional reaction to unfolding events. Thinking negatively creates the primary limits that hold you back and is the foremost deficit you must overcome. To be successful, you must burst forcefully through your self-imposed limitations and your love of your familiar routine. You do this by maximizing the talents and abilities you possess right this minute.

A final but important thought: You must think and act differently in everyday life. You will never be a high achiever by following your particular crowd of peers. If you think and act like your peers, then you will almost certainly obtain similar outcomes (which is usually financial scarcity). I believe in you, but much more importantly, believe in yourself and your abilities to accomplish your goals. It all starts with simply deciding to create financial wealth and then deciding to begin right now!

GOAL SETTING

Sub goals

CREATE TIMETABLE

DEVISE ACTION PLAN

RESEARCH

CREATE SUB-GOALS TO MARK YOUR PROGRESS AND AS BENCHMARKS FOR CELEBRATION!

WRITE YOUR GOALS (WHAT DO I REALLY WANT)

EVALUATE WHERE YOU STAND

Write Out Your Goal Plan

GOAL   TIME

ACTION STEPS

SUB-GOAL TIME

SUB-GOAL TIME

ZZZz

DON'T FOLLOW THE CROWD
TO FINANCIAL SCARCITY

4

Create Income

"Both poverty and riches are the offspring of thought."
—Napoleon Hill

Congratulations! You've set goals and now you're ready to take the next stair step to your financial independence. Right now, you're probably thinking, "I wish I'd win the lottery so I don't have to go to work," or, "I wish I had a vacation coming up," or, "I wish I was retired." Remember, a job is simply a means to an end. You have to earn money somehow—preferably legally. You need a job, whether that means being self-employed or working for someone else. How quickly you can quit your current job depends on how well you manage your money and master the steps required to build significant wealth.

Generating income is the second stair step to wealth creation. As you recall from Chapter 3, the stair steps to wealth and financial independence include goal-setting, income creation, budgeting, saving and then investing the money you saved. Without income, you cannot begin your climb to financial independence.

I don't like being told what to do. I'm not alone. Most people don't enjoy being told what to do. So working at a job can only be so appealing to human beings. Studies have conclusively proved the premise that if you enjoy doing a task and you do it now for free, your view of this activity will radically change if that task suddenly becomes your job. Once you are paid to do the activity, your interest in this pursuit begins to significantly decline. This is called the over-justification effect[1]. Therefore, even under the best of circumstances, a job can only be so appealing to humans.

The problem remains, however, that if you don't have a large pile of money to generate passive income, then you need to have a job until you can create that large pile of money. Many people fail to understand the real purpose of a job. Some might believe the purpose of a job is to make the world a better place via your efforts, energy and many talents. Altruism is excellent when it occurs, but that is not the actual purpose of your job. If that were the case, you could quit your job and volunteer 40 or more hours a week. Obviously, you can't do that and have any kind of decent lifestyle unless you're already financially independent. Income is absolutely essential to existence in our modern life.

Here is a good example: most police officers went into law enforcement because they really wanted to help people. They also felt their personalities were a good match for some of the action-oriented tasks required in this job. Many have wanted to do the job since they were small children. They loved their job at first. About three to five years later, new officers typically begin to experience serious burnout. If they can't find a way to get past career burnout, they end up quitting. Only those with emotional maturity are able to push past the burnout and thrive in the policing field.

The burnout phenomenon occurs in all fields. For example, even doctors face serious burnout and frequently migrate into related fields that don't require patient care. Remember, this was their dream job! They studied for years and years and completed long post-graduate work in residencies and sometimes fellowships to become doctors and treat the sick. This job is what they desperately wanted. However, a job is just a job. It is certainly better if you like it; and even better if it provides a service to mankind. But few people cheer (at least not for long) because they are headed to work.

The World Health Organization lists job burnout as a real medical condition. It is prevalent in almost every profession[2]. Burnout is caused by unresolved stress and the requirements of meeting other's expectations at your job—sometimes an impossible task to accomplish. This is true of doctors, lawyers, engineers, police officers, social workers, nurses, teachers, firefighters and most other professions that involve unresolved stress. When you primarily deal with other people, unresolved stress is your constant companion. These professionals must push past the roadblocks or they simply won't last in their careers.

Now, here is the interesting part. I became financially independent long before I retired from policing. In other words, I no longer needed my job to support my family or myself. The day it irritated me enough that I did not want to do it any longer, I could simply turn in my equipment and go home—forever. Surprisingly, I didn't leave. I stayed for a few more years. The reason I stayed on at my job when I no longer had to do so was because the majority of the stress and drudgery simply fell away when I knew I could quit at any time. Work became fun again. The burnout dissipated when I no longer felt I was forced to do it. I was able to relentlessly innovate, a creative endeavor I enjoy, and I dragged the entire organization along with me, with the help and consent of the chief.

The last years on the job, I had a great time. I never feared my innovations would fail because there was virtually no downside for me anymore. I stayed quite a few years until it became irritating to me. Once it did, I simply left by retiring—creating another income stream via a modest pension. When I left, I felt very satisfied with my career and my many accomplishments. I'd made the lives of the citizens in my city better. If you want to have the ability to choose to stay at a job only as long as you wish and then leave it, keep reading.

The medical field does a great deal of research on physician burnout and depression. There are several techniques physicians recommend to their peers to fight burnout, including exercising to reduce stress, reducing alcohol intake and eating healthier. Another suggestion they recommend to fight burnout and depression is to increase your wealth and reduce your debt. This makes physicians feel more independent and makes them feel like they have more options and choices in life[3]. Options and choices are the keys to prevent feelings of being trapped and "forced" to work at a job.

Even if you had your dream job, it would only be so exciting and gratifying. There would be parts of the job you would like and other parts you would hate. A job is about income, which gives you the quality of life you experience both now and in the future. A higher income gives you more choices and additional options. A lower income, even if your job helps society, significantly narrows your life options and lessens your satisfaction with your overall life situation.

WORLD HEALTH ORGANIZATION SAYS BURNOUT IS REAL

NO MATTER HOW MUCH YOU LIKE YOUR JOB, YOU SOON TIRE OF THE STRESS *AND* REQUIREMENTS OF WORK. THAT *CAN* *LEAD TO BURNOUT!*

FINANCIAL INDEPENDENCE CAN CREATE OPTIONS AND CHOICES!

5

Create Income: Ramping Up Your Income

"Formal education will make you a living; self-education
will make you a fortune."
—Jim Rohn

You should save at least 20 percent of your pay to create wealth in the future. I frequently hear from students in my classes, "I don't make enough money to save any part of my paycheck, let alone 20 percent of it." I call this the "prisoner mentality." You can become a prisoner of your past experiences. You can get stuck there and be unable to think beyond your past disappointments. My wife and I both experienced the harsh reality of low financial means, but we did not allow this past to dictate our future.

At times, we all seem to suffer from the "prisoner mentality." We get stuck in the past: past disappointments, past failures, past childhood pain, past poor relationships and past grudges. These negative emotions hold us back from achieving our goals. I can get stuck in the past as well. Luckily, I have a great support group that includes my wife, very smart adult children and great friends who help me re-adjust my thinking.

How do you leave negative emotions behind and create a brighter future? The same way you accomplish everything else worth doing—by goal-setting. List the things you are trying to get past and set goals to get that job done. Seek medical, psychiatric and/or legal assistance if that is what you require. The only way to create a better future is through goal-setting and working the necessary plan(s) to achieve your goals. That plan is preferable to "just seeing how it goes."

My lovely wife Lisa and I have a blended family. We got together when our children were very young. When we began our life together, we could barely save one hundred dollars a paycheck. What separated us from our peers was that we refused to allow our low financial existence to become our permanent reality. We set goals and aggressively worked to achieve them. By the time we were done, we were saving a full 50 percent of our pay and still had plenty of money to live very comfortably. When your total monthly financial resources represent a much larger pot, saving 50 percent really isn't as much of a chore as you might think.

However, to be able to save 20 percent or more, you will likely need to make more money. Caution! When most of your peers increase their income, they proportionally increase their expenses as well. This is the path most people take and it is the path that usually leads to financial scarcity in the future. This is also the well-trodden path to volunteer slavery. You are forever forced to work harder and harder just to keep servicing your family's growing debt. Reject the norm of increasing your expenses in proportion to your expanding income. Seek to live frugally.

I now volunteer at the local jail where I teach financial literacy to inmates. I explain to the inmates that they are not prisoners of their past. When they are released, they can create their own economic futures. I know that some of them don't believe me, so I go on to explain that many ex-convicts have become legitimate millionaires. I give the prisoners what I call my Quick 20 List. This is a list of 20 ex-convicts who started small businesses and eventually became legitimate millionaires. There are literally hundreds and hundreds of them. I stop at 20 because it more than proves my point. If these men and women can achieve financial independence with the problems they faced daily, then you can certainly achieve your financial goals. After all, creating financial independence is nowhere near as hard as serving time in jail!

To get rich as soon as possible, you will need to significantly ramp up your monthly income, which will allow you to save large amounts of money. For the many people supporting themselves with a job, here are four basic ways to ramp up income:

1. Get a raise from your current employer or by jumping to a new job with a higher paying employer.
2. Get a side job to make more money.
3. Start a small business as a side gig that might later become your primary job.
4. Create or join a startup business.

Side note: To create wealth for today and tomorrow that will reduce your stress and give you immediate financial means, you must create an emergency fund that can pay your bills for a year or more without employment (see Chapter 11). The knowledge that you have a financial buffer helps to embolden your thinking and career aggressiveness, while decreasing feelings of being trapped in any particular job!

The first winning strategy to increase your income is to use your current employer to maximize the pay and the benefits you receive for your considerable time and effort at work. This usually involves meeting and exceeding assigned goals, as well as taking on extra work throughout the year. In other words, you strive to make yourself invaluable. Increase your skills to increase both your abilities and marketability. Focus on the technical sides of your job and get good at it. Remember to always keep a running log of your accomplishments for your review period.

You can also keep your eye out for openings at similar companies to possibly snag a similar job with higher pay. Just keep in mind there is little point in jumping jobs for a small pay increase, unless the new job offers substantially more advancement opportunities. The hassles and expense of changing employers (for a small raise) is not usually worth the effort needed to create the change. As you increase your income over time, you can speed your path to wealth. As you obtain more pay, roll your raises straight into your savings and investing plan, which will significantly increase your portfolio size over time. This technique lessens the pain of saving a full 20 percent or more of your salary.

Getting promoted in the organizational chain is also a solid strategy to make more money. The higher you can climb, the higher your salary. Another benefit of getting promoted is you gain more freedom regarding how you will do your job. To go up the organizational structure usually requires a mix of talents that include the ability to navigate office politics, the right educational and training qualifications and garnering excellent job performance reviews. Accomplishing organizational upward movement is a full-time job and will require extra time and energy on your part. Continual self-improvement is required to grow in your organization. This technique will also require persistence and patience on your part.

The next strategy has been popularized as the "side gig" and involves simply getting a part-time job in addition to your regular job. Getting a side gig is probably the easiest of all the methods to increase your pay. This also exposes you to new business methods and increases your work skills. Save the extra income to cover your 20 percent savings goal.

Two of the riskier strategies to create wealth include leaving your current job and creating a startup, or joining a startup. Startup companies, both low-tech and high-tech, have made their founders and the first-in workers incredibly rich. The vast majority, however, sputter and fail. A full 80 percent are not in operation by the second year[1]. Most startups are home businesses and a third are started with less than $5,000 and are organized as a Limited Liability Company (LLC)[2]. This is an excellent organization structure and a good compromise between a very complicated corporate structure and the extensive liability of a sole proprietorship. LLCs offer their owners very limited liability should something go wrong, as long as you follow all the business rules for LLCs.

The reason why most startup fail is that the founders did not complete basic tasks necessary for starting a small business. For example, most startups have no business plan, they don't understand who their customers are, they don't understand how to obtain customers and they have no real marketing or operational plan. There is much to learn when starting and running a new business. Many believe that starting and running a small business is cheaper than a formal education and provides more practical and useful knowledge. Nevertheless, with proper research and a set business plan, starting a business on the side can extensively increase your skill sets.

Excellent, free or low-cost business training classes (even personal mentors) are offered by your local SCORE (Service Corp of Retire Executives) office. SCORE is a non-profit organization that is dedicated to educating future business owners. My personal experience with this organization has been very gratifying. For the record, I have several friends who achieved the goal of becoming successful small business owners. They became at least semi-rich and generated significant income. None of them achieved overnight success. They spent years and years learning and then perfecting their skills before they became successful. The experiences of these business owners are shining examples of the very important principle of luck meets preparation.

If you just don't care to get a second job, get promoted or start your own business, then you can concentrate on the budgeting end of this puzzle, combined with overtime at work. Learn to budget wisely, live frugally and save big. Smart budgeting and reducing your expenses will allow you to accomplish your goal.

In exchange for your time and labor, you are paid by your employer. How much you make significantly impacts your lifestyle and your ability to obtain wealth in your future. Working very hard early in your life paves the path for working less later in your life. Therefore, it is in your best interest to obtain as much as the market will bear for your labor, energy and time.

EASIER TO SAVE IF YOU KEEP YOUR
EXPENSES LOW & INCREASE INCOME!

4 BASIC WAYS TO RAMP UP YOUR INCOME:

1. GET A RAISE FROM YOUR EMPLOYER OR COMPETING COMPANY VIA A NEW JOB

2. GET A SIDE JOB/ SIDE HUSTLE

3. CREATE A SIDE BUSINESS

4. JOIN OR CREATE A STARTUP

6

Budgeting: Live a Different Lifestyle

"Whenever you find yourself on the side of the majority,
it is time to pause and reflect."
—Mark Twain

Congratulations! You've set your goals, found ways to create income stream(s) and have made it to the next stair step toward financial independence—creating a budget. Living by a budget is not the norm in America. Most people live paycheck to paycheck with few spending controls and little to no financial planning. Only about 32 percent of Americans even bother with setting and writing out a budget[1]. Your dedication to your budget and your goals, however, is what separates you from this crowd of financial low-achievers. Of course, this requires living a different type of lifestyle than your peers.

Begin your budgeting journey with an understanding of the Tyrannical Rule of Money, which states that you must control your money or your money will certainly control you. Money does not care about you in any conceivable way! It flows through all parts of your life and its power over your life is inescapable. It can lift you up or it can destroy you just as easily. There is no compromising with money.

In previous chapters, I talked about having the courage to live a different kind of life than your peers. The life I am talking about is a life of winning the inner battle with both yourself and money's seductive power to wantonly spend it. Living frugally by choice is truly the road less traveled. The heart of this money problem is it's very easy to outspend your income. It can be so much fun to bust your monthly budget! Even rich people outspend their budgets all the time. Movie stars, highly paid athletes and celebrities go broke every day. This is especially true if they didn't make their money over time and instead, obtained sudden wealth, like a lottery winner, or, in the case of new athletes, struck it big all at once. They did not develop the ground-level skills required to manage their money as they dramatically increased their wealth.

Right now you are thinking that most of this book is about pinching pennies so hard your fingers bleed. I won't lie, the initial shock of changing your lifestyle is kind of rough for beginners. Here is something most other personal finance books never tell you. After only a short time, if you stick with it, it's not a big deal anymore and involves minimal discomfort.

Here are seven reasons why budgeting won't bother you after only a few years:

1. You will make more and more money as each year passes.
2. As you make more money, a larger percentage is available to fund day-to-day luxuries.
3. You adjust to budgeting as a normal part of your life and it no longer creates anxiety.
4. In a few years you have paid down your debts so that it frees up more income for living your daily life.

5. You can place most of your budgeting actions on automatic pilot so that you don't have to think about this chore most of the time.

6. Your peers never bother to budget and debt soon takes over all facets of their lives and won't be able to go out with you for a night on the town anyway.

7. Your progress will make you feel great about your life and your new found independence.

So the pain you feel when you first start budgeting is temporary. A 2018 study by Charles Schwab Corporation showed that 43 percent of millennials are not living within their means and have gone into debt to pay their regular monthly bills[2], but failure to budget is not just a millennial issue. Based on the results of their 2017 wage earners' survey, the employment firm CareerBuilders reported that 78 percent of Americans live paycheck to paycheck[3]. Most people have significant debt and they expect to remain in debt their entire lives. This even occurs with workers who make over $100,000 annually.

You will either budget and create savings that will significantly improve all aspects of your life in the future or live frugally because you spent too much money and are now trying to stay afloat financially. One way or the other, budgeting is inevitable. Since that is the case, why not make living frugally count for something, like creating a future life of financial independence? Budgeting can dramatically change your financial situation for the better in only a few short years.

In our 40s, my wife and I could almost do anything we wanted to do, within reason. Most of our peers, however, were struggling with serious money issues. As our friends aged into their 60s, their money issues continued. Remember, it is very easy to outspend your income no matter how high it is. There will never be a day you can skip budgeting, even if you become very wealthy. The very definition of budgeting is controlling your income. You put considerable time, energy and stress into creating that income, and it should be honored. Budgeting will make sure that your work counts for something—both today and tomorrow.

Budgeting always begins with recording your income and listing every dime you spend for a couple of months. I used the notes section on my phone for this task. You can't build a budget unless you know your basic income and expense numbers. Don't be embarrassed by or afraid of those numbers. Everyone has to start somewhere.

I am a proponent of utilizing the 50/30/20 budget mix. This particular budget mix was made popular by Elizabeth Warren in a book she co-authored with Amelia Warren-Tyagi, *All Your Worth: The Ultimate Lifetime Money Plan[4]*. This book will provide significant benefits if you take the information and integrate it into your life.

The 50/30/20 budget mix includes using 50 percent of your take-home pay (after taxes) to cover your "needs" or regular monthly bills and all expenses for food, clothing, shelter, debt and transportation. Then use 30 percent toward your expenses in the "wants" category, which covers rewards for living by your budget, such as eating out, entertainment and buying something special you desire within budget limits. The remaining 20 percent should be routed into your savings and investing plan. The following is a further breakdown of the 50/30/20 budgeting plan:

The 50 percent category covers basic needs:

- Mortgage/rent
- Insurance(s)

- Utilities (level billing if possible)
- Transportation
- Student loan
- Child support
- Groceries
- Haircuts
- Clothes (basic only)
- Babysitting required to cover your work time
- Debt repayment

The 30 percent category covers the things you want/rewards for following budget:

- Eating at a restaurant/entertainment
- Hobbies
- Coffee at a coffee shop (rather than coffee at home)
- Cable/streaming service (Netflix/Hulu/Prime)
- Vehicle improvements (anything beyond basic repairs)
- Groceries (any items beyond basic foods)
- Babysitting (any time not required for work)
- Gas (any travel other than required)
- Any special clothing items

The 30 percent reward category is used to go out and have fun or to purchase something outside your needs (50 percent category). If you have trouble and go over your budget in some other category, this is the category you pull from first. This helps create a self-correcting loop that makes you pay attention to your numbers and gives you an incentive to stay within your budget parameters.

The 20 percent category is for putting 20 percent of your pay into savings (see Chapter 11).

Many people stress out over writing a budget. If you're one of them, there are some reasonably good work-arounds. You can try mapping your budget. Draw a chart with a box labeled "Income" at the top with the map flowing downward to a box labeled "Life." On the left side of the Income box, list items from the 50 percent needs category. On the right side of the box, list items from your 30 percent wants category. Both sets of expenses flow into the Life box along with your income. Your hard-earned savings drop from the bottom of the Life box.

Another strategy is to only work on your budget for about 15 minutes at a stretch each day. This method reduces any feelings of dread and apprehension. The strategy of setting up your monthly bills to be paid automatically online from your checking account automates most of the routine budget tasks and takes the burden of monthly bill paying off your shoulders. That way, you can primarily manage your wants category. The same strategy of using automatic money routing can be used for savings. You can route your savings into various savings/investing accounts before you ever see it.

In my book, *Messages From Your Future: The Seven Rules for Financial, Personal and Professional Success*[5], I advocated for achieving financial independence early in life. I explained in that book that your present actions travel outward through time and create your future—either a positive or negative future. The same can be said about personal finances. Your present action or inaction regarding your personal budget will create your future. What kind of future will you create for yourself?

MONTHLY 50/30/20 BUDGET MAP

INCOME

LIST
50% NEEDS

LIST
30% WANTS

YOUR
LIFE

20%

20%
SAVINGS

7

Budget: The Why and the How of the Tasks Ahead

"How many millionaires do you know who have become wealthy by investing in savings accounts? I rest my case."
—Robert G. Allen

Would you like to earn between $40,000 to $50,000 a year and not have to go to work to get paid? You can earn this money by building your nest egg and putting it to work as a passive income stream generator! Here's how:

<u>Goal:</u> Create a minimum of $1,000,000 in a portfolio of various investments that you will use to generate passive income later. That large nest egg can easily generate $40,000 to $50,000 in annual income on average for your use and still allow your portfolio of investments to continue to grow. It is the power of large numbers, time and compounding interest that will create your passive income-producing machine.

Just follow along and you will understand exactly what the task entails and why we use certain methods to achieve our goals.

Below are annual salary ranges multiplied by 30 years (the average work career) to give you an idea of your expected total lifetime earnings. When we compare these numbers, it will give us a good idea of the job ahead.

$35,000 annually x 30 years = $1,050,000
$51,000 annually x 30 years = $1,530,000
$61,000 annually x 30 years = $1,841,160 (average income bracket in 2017)
$85,000 annually x 30 years = $2,550,000
$110,000 annually x 30 years = $3,300,000
$150,000 annually x 30 years = $4,500,000

You must pay all your bills and expenses during your working lifetime with these earnings. Don't forget, however, that there will be many years to pay bills when you are not working, making the income you are earning today important for your present and future needs.

According to a U.S. Census Bureau report, the median household income as reported by our last census (2017) was $61,372[1]. That would equal approximately $1,841,160 in lifetime earnings (see above). Note that it is almost impossible to physically save $1,000,000 from your lifetime salary total. You would have inadequate funds to cover everyday living expenses. This practical demonstration should be a wake-up call to those who only want to save and not invest their money. There is a better solution!

To get $1,000,000 portfolio, you need to begin not only saving but investing as well. We are discussing a 30-year period for this example, though you can certainly achieve your goal sooner. Luckily, you don't have to save $1,000,000 from your wages. In actual wages, my wife and I only saved and invested approximately a third of the money we now possess. To accomplish your goal, if you are in the average income range, you need only save one-third of your million dollar target. If your goal is $1,000,000, you must save roughly $333,333 over your working career. This money is invested over time (see Chapter 13) to achieve the total you are aiming for. Our experience in this area is very consistent with others we know who have also accomplished this goal.

Of course, salaries are never static. Most people actually travel through the income scales and continue to earn more every year. I call this phenomenon the lifetime earnings arc. You make more each year until you are in your early 60s, then your salary levels off. This is likely because you will be at the top of the pay scale for your career field.

Ageism is alive and well in the American workplace. A 2018 AARP report on ageism shows that 56 percent of older employees (over age 50) are forced out of the company or forced to retire early[2]. You must either find another job at a drastically reduced pay rate or simply retire. Additionally, women are usually forced out much sooner than men, so sexism is also a factor in job tenure issues. Today, women typically still make 25 percent less than men. This information tells us that our ability to earn money is limited. We will receive a finite amount of money during our working careers. Let that sink in. Regardless of who you are, your future earnings are limited. It is likely a very tangible and easily calculable amount. Most people don't understand this vital concept. How you utilize the income you receive is critical to your future.

For the next piece of the puzzle, we will use the Million-Dollar Savings Calculator[3] to prove that you need only save one-third of $1,000,000 to create your investment nest egg. This calculator utilizes compound interest to project the result. You input the number of years you have to save and at what interest rate you anticipate receiving on your investments. For my calculation, I kept the interest rate a relatively conservative six percent. My wife and I actually ended up doing better than six percent and were closer to 10 percent over our investing lifetime. According to the Million-Dollar Savings Calculator, 30 years at six percent would require you to save $995.50 a month. The cost of total savings in actual dollars equals $358,200 over a 30-year period, which is roughly one-fifth or just under 20 percent of your lifetime earnings total of approximately $1,855,740 (assuming an average salary). Experiment with this calculator to see how much you need to save over shorter or longer periods of time.

If you can't save 20 percent of your income, I totally understand your predicament, but you can work up to that amount over time. I started by saving only $50 a month. I soon went to saving $100 a month, then $150 and so on. I took the steps described in this book to get to the 20 percent goal. We were eventually saving well beyond the 20 percent figure. Because you will likely make more than six percent interest, building your monthly savings over time is a proven successful strategy. The sooner you start saving, the easier this task will be.

Accomplishing this goal is a matter of priority. If you are committed, there is very little that can stop you for long. By the time I retired from the police department, my wife and I were saving over 50 percent of our combined wages. This is not unusual for high financial achievers. You can do this as well!

8

Budget: Finances and Your Significant Other

"A good husband makes a good wife."
—John Florio

Money problems are one of the top reasons couples split according to a recent survey of married couples. The results of that survey are not surprising[1]. When conflict between couples regarding money arise, the root cause is most likely because financial goals were never agreed upon, have been forgotten or one or more partners lacks the motivation to make the shared goals happen.

If I had my way, before couples got together, they would be required to have a formal "reveal" ceremony in which the partners would exchange financial summary sheets to have a complete financial picture of the person they love. That way, at the very least, both individuals would understand exactly what they were getting into with the new union. A financial reveal ceremony would also make finances much more important to single people looking for long-term relationships. Unfortunately, the financial analysis of your potential mate often occurs way too late to be of any value. Couples are left to figure these things out after they are already married or living together. My reveal concept is not very romantic, so I really don't see my reveal ceremony becoming popular in the near future. But, then again, what could be more romantic than ensuring your future partner that you value your financial security?

You must decide upon and create shared goals with your soul mate. During the various classes I teach on personal finance, I talk with so many people who tell me they agree with my curriculum, but their spouse is not compliant with the family budgeting and savings program. These people are frustrated and some are even downright angry and resentful.

Adding to the difficulty of agreeing on shared goals is the very real pressure we have to follow our peers and enjoy the same lifestyle. Not following the crowd can have one or both partners feeling alienated from their friends because they are being left out. Doing the same thing everyone else does, however, will likely lead to limited financial resources.

The best way to get couples on the same page financially is to discuss and set long-term, mid-term and short-term financial goals. If the goals are both valued and shared, both people will be willing to work and sacrifice to achieve those goals. If not, it will be a difficult journey forward.

A person's values are learned from their family and their larger culture and/or sub-culture. From these values we construct the goals that are important to us. Since backgrounds are diverse, you might think you will face serious challenges in the areas of shared values. Surprisingly, however, most families and cultures share values like honesty, integrity, learning, ambition and per-severance. So the job of creating goals from shared values is not as hard as you might initially believe. Values heavily influence a person's motivation to achieve goals. If a partner doesn't value the goal, it's not important and will not become a priority. Values do change over time, but they typically do so slowly as a result of life experiences and/or new sub-culture identifications.

What happens so many times is a partner gets upset at the money behavior of his or her significant other. The emotional turmoil that ensues usually leads both partners to raising their voices and speaking in harsh words, which is unlikely to change anyone's long-term behavior. In fact, constantly using this issue to berate your partner may lead to your relationship dissolving. According to psychologists, you need five positive interactions to every negative interaction you have with your significant other[2]. If you start to drop below that ratio, your relationship starts to deteriorate.

What you cannot do is harass your partner into better money behaviors. He or she is a separate living person who you cannot control; at least not for very long. Giving someone serious heat for not living up to the budget might work in the short-term, but will never create the lasting behaviors you will need to accomplish your shared goals. You can, however, positively influence his or her behavior through leadership and exhibiting a great attitude!

So, how do you get your partner to take the issue of achieving financial goals more seriously? To understand, let's not view finances as a potential conflict, but, rather, a leadership opportunity to motivate your partner to enact better budgetary and savings behaviors.

Leadership in the area of finance begins with your own behavior. Demonstrate the behavior you want to see from your partner with your own actions. You also need to be positive and able to freely discuss money issues without getting upset or trying to skirt the truth. If you fail to demonstrate the behavior you want to see, your efforts will have little influence over your partner and will be seen as, "Do as I say and not as I do." All of us are typically great at finding behaviors that need improvement with our partners, but not always so great at recognizing our own errant behaviors. You should try to be bulletproof in the areas of budgeting, spending and saving.

Now that we are more attuned to our own behaviors, we can begin to try to influence the behavior of our significant other. Gráinne M. Fitzsimons and Eli J. Finkel have researched the area of partner motivation thoroughly. They conclude that you can help increase your significant other's commitment to your shared goals— assuming you both did the work together to create shared goals[3]. The strategies you use, however, are very important.

You are trying to motivate your significant other. Motivation, just like at work, is best accomplished by thoroughly explaining the benefits of achieving the goal and then both encouraging and recognizing your partner's progress toward achieving this vision. After all, you share this vision and you should both feel excitement for it. Give praise and recognition for his or her efforts regularly. Also, be forgiving! We all make mistakes and have epic failures. Treat your significant other like you would want to be treated if you'd made a mistake. Speaking harshly or belittling your partner will create resentments that will live long after this particular issue is forgotten.

Another leadership principle (after demonstrating the correct behaviors and praising your partner frequently) is helping him or her to develop strategies to improve performance. If your partner will accept it, provide this assistance on strategies in a positive, subtle manner. If he or she starts to get resentful, lay off the issue for a bit. Let it be known that you are there to help and wait for your partner to approach you. Don't overly intrude into your significant other's behaviors. If your help is not requested or wanted, this will only lead to increased resentment and further relationship obstacles. You have already discussed the monthly budget spending parameters when they were initially set. Wait until the end of month to make any comments, which should be phrased in the following manner: "How can I help you achieve _____?"

Some people say, "My significant other is smart, and he or she will know I am trying to manipulate them with this strategy." Yes! Your partner may know exactly what you are doing, but that doesn't mean it won't work. This is also an effective strategy in the workplace that you've likely already participated in. You try to achieve your work organization's goals because you value the relationship you have with both your organization and your boss. A similar—or stronger—bond should exist with domestic partners.

Even so, some partners may hide the truth about finances, avoid telling the whole story or downright lie. If this is a chronic behavior, it is a very serious problem. If discussion (not yelling) does not improve or stop the behavior, it will require professional counseling for the two of you. If this behavior is surfacing with money, then it's possible other areas of the marriage aren't working as well.

As discussed in previous chapters, we all overcome obstacles on our journey to goal achievement. This is just another bump on the road. You and your partner can be successful by discovering shared values, creating shared goals and then by sharing the work and sacrifices needed to achieve those goals.

MONEY ISSUES ARE THE #2 REASON COUPLES SPLIT:

1. SET SHARED GOALS

2. IMPROVE YOUR OWN BEHAVIOUR FIRST

3. ENCOURAGE & MOTIVATE YOUR PARTNER

4. TREAT YOUR PARTNER LIKE YOU WANT TO BE TREATED IF YOU MADE A MISTAKE

5. DON'T LIE OR MISLEAD

6. GET HELP IF PROBLEMS PERSIST.

9

Budget: Do You Want to be a Financial Winner or a Loser?

"Unless you do something beyond what you have already
mastered, you will never grow."
—Ronald E. Osborn

Just as I have seen many people achieve great financial success, I
have seen others fail horribly with money. I have witnessed people make so many poor financial decisions that their day-to-day lives become miserable. They have no money, and if they actually obtained any money it would be taken away by the courts or their creditors. These were real couples who lived in our neighborhood, and they lost their houses, got divorced and their lives spiraled increasingly out of control. They ended up angry, negative and usually blamed others for their misfortune.

I have known individuals who had steady jobs, but their personal problems so overwhelmed them they could not maintain control of their finances and later found themselves jobless and destitute. This happened far too often with people at work. In an attempt to scratch their persistent itch of personal unhappiness, they made terrible financial decisions. I saw this happen so many times I actually recognized the warning signs when the spiral began. Talking with the troubled people seemed to have no impact on what seemed to be a determined downward spiral.

Most people, no matter how long they have been working, have less than $25,000 in liquid financial assets[1]. All their years of hard work and effort end up counting for next to nothing. Sure, they are able to live their day-to-day lives, but they have no extra money and few options in life. Their futures become bleak and limited. It's hard to imagine having $25,000 or less and a ton of debt at the end of a 25- or 30-year career. Once you accept the ironclad rule that you alone are responsible for most of your bad economic outcomes, it allows you the freedom to make different, better and bolder choices.

The majority of the population does not bother to set financial goals, let alone set the goal of becoming financially independent. Failing to set goals is the first major hindrance to financial success. Brokerage house Charles Schwab reports that only one in four Americans have any kind of written financial plan[2]. Without a plan, you'll soon arrive at the popular destination of Nowhere in Particular.

Even a rough financial plan in your head is inadequate for the job of creating any kind of financial independence. A rough plan is not detailed, not backed by necessary research and you don't have a clear view of what the strategies are or how to apply them in your life to achieve your goals. Goal-setting is always the first step in accomplishing any personal, athletic, financial or career-related ambition in your life. As my very smart wife always says, "Plan ahead to get ahead."

A lack of knowledge about financial principles is a huge barrier to becoming financially independent. Americans (in particular) are rarely trained in even basic finance skills. Most schools do not cover the subject during the entire 12 years of primary education. Unfortunately, parents rarely know enough to be effective teachers at home, so the job never gets done correctly. For example, most parents are still stuck in the paradigm that you should go to college—at any cost. That belief has simply proven to be untrue in our modern world. How much college debt you carry forward is extremely important. Paying too much for college creates financial havoc and limits your options for the rest of your life. You can end up with so much college debt you can never pay it off, especially if the degree is in a field with low pay. This keeps you in working class poverty almost forever.

Financial education is so bad in our country that the Program for International Student Assessment rates Americans seventh out of the top 15 developed countries in financial literacy[3]. Additionally, only 30 percent of Americans feel they have enough financial knowledge to achieve their goals[4]. This creates a financial knowledge crisis that severely impacts family outcomes and creates significant hardship throughout all stages of life. It doesn't have to be that way.

The worst part of this educational neglect is that basic personal finance principles and skills are not difficult to learn. In fact, they are relatively easy to master. Even though I have encouraged you to educate yourself, you must be very careful about what you read and take in. An entire financial industry that includes scammers is dedicated to taking your money. If someone is trying to convince you of a particular financial path, you may want to ask yourself what is his or her motivation? How does this information benefit you? How does this information benefit the person giving it to you?

Middle-class workers are not the only ones who have money management issues. Doctors, lawyers and police chiefs rarely receive any personal finance training. They just seem wealthier because they are usually working with a larger pot of money than most of us. I have taught many personal finance classes to doctors and lawyers. If you start looking at the percentage of money spent versus money saved and invested, you can see that the majority of high earners perform just as dismally as the general population.

Poor money management skills, flowing from a lack of financial literacy, create poor individual choices and needless financial scarcity. In the area of personal finances, knowledge is power. In fact, knowledge is the absolute king of the personal financial hill! Without a baseline of basic finance knowledge, you can't make sound choices.

Even with a decent job and good pay, most people are not financially successful because they inhabit a mental prison that is entirely self-constructed, which holds them back psychologically from taking another path and thinking differently than their peers. They just can't envision making bold choices to create wealth. Most people never stop to consider that they can live a life that is tailor-made to fit them with plenty of financial resources to support that life with just a little planning, perseverance and work. They never seriously consider taking their own stair steps to financial independence. Even if they could picture their unique version of a perfect life, many are not willing to pay the entry price required to achieve this goal, which is simply sustained effort over time. Some are just too lazy, while others lack the commitment necessary to create and follow through on any financial plan. If your financial goals aren't a priority, then they are simply a daydream or wish.

Another common problem is that so many people procrastinate

in the area of budgeting, saving and investing. Everyone knows they should be saving, but most plan on doing it tomorrow, next month or next year. The dates keep getting pushed back, and real progress toward financial goals never happens. When should you start saving? Actually, the best time was several years ago. The next best time is today! Some high achievers started when they were kids. The earlier you start, the easier this whole process becomes. Not that you can't accomplish the goal if you start now, it just requires more effort and focus on your part. The website investopedia.com reports[5] that if you procrastinate until the age of 45, you will have to save three times as much as a person who started at age 25[6].

It is an absolute tragedy that the average person now equates saving money with the task of saving for retirement. Equating savings to retirement allows us to procrastinate. Retirement seems like such a distant future event that it may never occur. The financial industry has so effectively and persuasively linked saving and retirement together through marketing, that the two concepts seem to be forever linked in the minds of the American public.

From my perspective, financial independence has little if anything to do with retirement. A comfortable retirement is just one of the many perks of becoming financially independent—but it is not the goal. As stated earlier, financial independence is defined as accumulating financial wealth to a point where you no longer require a traditional job to support yourself while living your chosen lifestyle and occurs when you put enough thought and persistent effort into the tasks necessary to achieve your goal.

Most people do what I call running with the herd. They do exactly the same things they see their peers doing. They hang out with friends at Starbucks, spend money on expensive cars, pay too much for their homes or rent and purchase boats, motorcycles, vacation homes and expensive luxuries. They procrastinate on saving until some future date. As time progresses, they just figure they will work a little longer and continue to put off saving.

Another reason that people don't become financially independent is that they are mired in dysfunctional relationships or relationships that drain all the positive energy from them. Their relationships dominate their lives to the point that they literally suck away most of their ambition and happiness. Toxic relationships (or downright abusive relationships) with a spouse, significant other or family members, and the accompanying drama, hold so many people back from the success in life they desire.

You can overcome the impact of these toxic relationships in your life by consciously choosing to reduce relationship drama and stress today! In some cases, it may be necessary to save yourself by discarding toxic and drama-ridden relationships altogether, which is painful, but at least the pain becomes much duller over time. If this is one of the problems you must overcome, I recommend a counselor to help you with this burden.

Examining the reasons people fail to become financially independent gives us great insight on our own paths to success and wealth. The stair steps to financial independence are fairly simple. From your needs, values and desires, you set appropriate and positive goals. You do the research to gain the knowledge you need to succeed. You create an action plan to achieve each goal, understanding it will take effort to succeed. You overcome problems that you will inevitably encounter along the way by keeping a positive attitude. You also understand that you will rarely succeed by following the crowd. The results you are seeking are much greater than the ones obtained by the vast majority of people. You can do this! After all, reading this book is your first step of your journey to financial achievement.

AFTER YEARS OF HARD WORK, LITTLE TO SHOW FOR IT IS THE NORM

BUDGET AND LIVE FRUGALLY NOW OR
YOU WILL JUST END UP BUDGETING LATER
TO SERVICE YOUR HUGE DEBT

BETTER PATH

1. SET FINANCIAL GOALS
2. EDUCATE YOURSELF
3. THINK & ACT DIFFERENTLY THAN PEERS
4. DON'T BE LAZY
5. TAKE CARE OF PERSONAL LIFE
6. DON'T PROCRASTINATE

10

Budget: Debt Monsters

"Remember that credit is money."
—Benjamin Franklin

Debt is a gargantuan, ugly monster that wreaks havoc wherever it goes. It destroys empires, drags down states, crushes cities and eats people for fun. Powerful people have kneeled or fled before its terrible power. When debt rears its ugly head, people run for their financial lives. There is no compromise with debt. Like money, you will either control your debt or it will control you.

Let's do a little math to illustrate the point. Let's say your monthly disposable income (take-home pay after taxes and other mandatory payroll deductions) is $4,064. To determine how much money to budget for your needs, take 50 percent of your monthly take-home pay: $4,064 x .50 = $2,032. The $2,032 number in this example should cover all your essential bills and include basic food, housing, clothing, utilities, transportation, phone and debt. If all your regular monthly bills are over 50 percent, you are beginning to run an increased risk of experiencing financial difficulties. Of course, what always suffers is the 20 percent savings category.

That may work in your present, but it does not work at all for your future. You are essentially robbing your future in exchange for money in the present. If you don't save money, you are creating long-lasting servitude to the debt monster and your monthly bills.

Now let's take it a step further and look at debt-to-income (DTI) ratio. All your debt (consumer loans, credit cards, car, personal loans, etc.) should be equal to or less than 36 percent of your monthly take-home pay. Let's say you have $1,300 in monthly debt payments that you pay from your $4,064 in monthly take-home salary. Using this example, calculate your DTI ratio by using this formula: your total debt (all monthly debt payments added together) divided by monthly take-home pay. This will equal your percentage of debt (after you multiply the answer by 100 to turn it into a percentage). Don't get nervous about the math, just grab your phone calculator and follow along:

- DTI = (all monthly debt payments/monthly take home pay) x 100
- Our example: $1,300 / $4,064 = .32.
- .32 x 100 and you get 32 percent.
- So 32 percent of your monthly take-home salary is your DTI ratio.

The person in this example is in good shape as far as DTI ratio. If your total debt is over 36 percent, creditors begin to tighten your credit. If your DTI ratio reaches around 43 percent, you will likely be denied a home mortgage and most creditors will stop lending you money at anything approaching a reasonable interest rate. Also, your risk of defaulting on your loan(s) substantially rises.

DTI ratio is not all you have to consider. Two key elements that impact your debt monster are interest rates and length of repayment. The interest rate charged on your debt can significantly increase the overall amount of money you pay over the life of the debt. Your FICO (Fair Isaac Corporation) score determines the interest rate the lender will charge you to borrow money. You earn (earn being the operative word) your FICO score based on your total debt, timely payments and your DTI ratio. A lender bases your interest rate on your FICO score. Typically, the better your FICO score, the lower your interest rate. The lower your interest rate, the less money you pay overall to borrow the money, which impacts your FICO score. This is obviously a vicious cycle. Keep your debt monster smaller by paying your bills on time!

The higher your interest rate on any particular loan, the higher the risk is to your personal finances. An eight percent loan is riskier to your financial health than a four percent loan because the payment on an eight percent loan is either much higher, or the payments last for a longer time period. Either way, the eight percent loan limits the amount of money you have to use for other purposes, like saving or eliminating your debt monster. For example, a mortgage loan is riskier than a car loan because something could happen over the longer duration of a mortgage loan that could prevent you from making timely payments.

Your long-term student loan can (and almost certainly will) create significant financial risk for your future. The long-term commitment of a student loan is one of the many reasons so many student loans are now in default. Student loans destroy financial lives by taking away or limiting a worker's early ability to save money, which reduces a worker's total net worth for his or her entire lifetime. Not being able to save money early in life sets you up to possibly become a virtual slave to debt and so many other money woes. Unfortunately, that is not all the harm student debt causes. Student debt can push your DTI ratio up so high that it damages your credit rating/FICO score. With a high DTI ratio, few if any, lenders will lend you money.

A poor credit rating impacts many other important facets of your life. For example, all employers run your credit rating/FICO score. If your DTI ratio is too high, you might be denied employment. The military won't allow you to go into their better job fields with a bad credit rating. A damaged credit rating will create a red flag on your military background check. You will not be able to obtain the proper security clearance rating required for the better military jobs—or even government contract jobs. Finally, landlords, car insurance companies and utility companies run your credit rating. A high DTI ratio might make it harder for you to find a place to live, and insurance for almost everything will cost you more. Many utility companies report your payment history to the credit bureaus, which can positively or negatively impact your credit rating/FICO score. By earning a better credit score, you earn lower payments on insurance and interest on credit cards and loans!

If you don't have school debt, then by all means avoid taking on any. Perhaps you could consider four years of military service. Past military service will allow you to save money during your enlistment. Once you finish your tour, the military will pay for your college and pay you a monthly stipend as you attend. Perhaps going to a community college for the first two years and then attending a cheaper (more cost-effective) state institution once you graduate from the community college is an option. You could also attend college part-time and work or find an employer that will provide you with tuition reimbursement.

Where you earned your degree makes absolutely no difference on a job application, unless attending Harvard or some other top-tier school that significantly impacts your career field. I have been on several hiring teams over my administrative career. We never refused to take a candidate based on which college they attended. If the college or university is properly accredited, no employers that I know of care what college you attended.

If you already have school debt, you are not alone. By the year 2020, student loans are expected to be the highest loan amount in America as the debt grows to over two trillion, surpassing car loans and credit card loans.

Try to find an employer who will help you pay down your school loan. Look for student loan forgiveness programs that will pay your tuition—up to a certain percentage. The federal government, for example, will pay part of your tuition if you agree to work for them in high-demand jobs and geographic areas for a required period of time (currently, this stands at three years). Nurses, lawyers, doctors and many other similar professions also have special programs for service in high-demand geographic areas in exchange for substantial tuition pay-downs. A ".gov" search in these areas can speed you along to freedom from your oppressive college debt!

Another debt monster that can derail your future is a pricey mortgage. So many people get wrapped up in where they live and in what kind of home. High mortgage balances are a threat to your future. Not only will it keep you poor in the present, but paying a high mortgage robs your future as well. Additionally, the more expensive your home, the harder it is to resell. An average-priced house in your geographic area will usually be the easiest home to resell and is also more likely to provide you with a lower DTI ratio. Your DTI ratio is critical! If you have a high DTI ratio, your future financial viability is at risk. A job loss, car accident, illness or

Larry Faulkner

downsizings at work might unexpectedly devastate your financial life. The rule is, the less debt you have, the more secure you are financially.

Which is the least expensive option for you: a six percent interest loan or a seven percent interest loan with the same repayment time period? If you answered six percent, you may be wrong. You actually do not have enough information to give an accurate answer. It all depends on the fees charged in each of these loans. Lenders can add so many fees on top of the interest rate that the true interest rate could actually be as high as 10 percent. Here are some common lending fees:

- Origination fee
- Application fee
- Processing fee
- Annual fee
- Funding fee
- Late fee
- Points (fees you pay to the lender to get a lower interest rate)

When your loan's fees are added into the percentage rate, it is called the Annual Percentage Rate or APR. The APR is usually higher than the lower interest rate lenders advertise. By law, however, lenders must eventually disclose to you their actual APR. When deciding upon a loan, use the APRs to compare loans rather than the simple advertised rate.

To decrease or eliminate your debt monster, start by reducing your Needs category and finding ways to eliminate or downsize. Can you live in a smaller apartment? Is there a way to reduce your utility usage? Can you sell some of the consumer items you purchased and use the proceeds to pay down or pay off your debt monster? Can you sell your expensive vehicle and buy something less costly?

In the Wants category, look hard at what is important to you and what you could easily live without. After that, look at what changes you can make in your lifestyle to reduce your spending in those areas that are important to you without adversely impacting your lifestyle. For example, my wife and I meet other couples and play trivia every Thursday evening. After a while, it became pretty expensive. Rather than eating dinner there every Thursday, we reduced our expenses by eating at home before we left. This was not a hardship because the restaurant food was expensive and not that great. My wife and I would then split an appetizer rather than buying two meals. We also limited ourselves to one alcoholic drink and then drank water the rest of the night. We barely noticed the changes, but cut our Thursday night bill by well over 50 percent.

If your debt monster and monthly Needs category have become dangerously high, you may have to forgo most items in your Wants category and probably your Savings category until you can get your finances back within normal category/percentage limits. There have been entire books written about getting out of debt. If that is a problem you face, grab one of them from your local library—using the library is a great way to save money.

A relatively new and useful application for your smart devices can be found at underbit.com. This site provides the users with various tools and an easy-to-understand analysis of the best course of actions the user can take to free themselves from burdensome debt[1]. You can use either the free version, or sign-up for the subscription version for $12.00 annually. Once you enter your information into the app, it displays various methodologies to get you out of debt.

The top two methods of debt reduction include the Snowball method, where you attack the smallest debt balance first, then the next smallest debt balance on the next loan, and so on. The avalanche method is the next most common method. This technique involves attacking the debt with the loan that has the highest interest rate first. After that is paid off, you then attack the loan with the next highest interest rate, and so on.

The app at undebtit.com also provides you with a spreadsheet and a timetable (based on the data you enter) for each of these methods to compare results[2]. It even includes an analysis of various hybrid methods of debt reduction. The value of this site is that it easily allows you to compare "what if" scenarios to free yourself from your own personal debt monster. With this app you can track and celebrate your progress toward clearing your debt.

The best budgeting applications for your smart devices include mint.com[3] and ynab.com[4]. Both are excellent budgeting tools. I prefer YNAB, as it seems easier to use and provides a better analysis of your budget. YNAB also uses colors to categorize expenses, which is more intuitive. Check these out if you want to carry your budget around with you for easy consultation and fast data entry in real time.

If you still need help, do your research and locate a reputable debt counseling service in your area. Be very careful and do your homework on the company. Many debt counseling companies market altruistic intentions to hide their profit-generating schemes. Read all the fine print. Look for hidden fees. Calculate what it will cost you overall versus what you will save. Using these companies to help you get out of debt may be a losing proposition. Once you pay the required fees for their assistance, they may or may not provide the needed help, which would be a shame, especially since that money could have gone to pay off some of your bills.

Everyone has faced hard financial times. Just remember, whatever happened yesterday remains in the past. It can't be changed now. What matters now is what you do today and tomorrow. You can suffer your whole life with limited financial means or you can take directed, informed and decisive actions to bring your debt monster and overall financial life under your control.

Remember, there are only two actions you can take when your monthly bills become too high. The first is to increase your income and the second is to reduce your debt. Many people who have become financially successful were initially in a worse situation than you find yourself in now. They became successful by getting their debt monster under control and then building wealth by creating savings for their investing program(s). If they did it, there is no reason you can't do it as well.

DEBT RISKS:

1. TOTAL DEBT BECOMES TOO LARGE
2. HIGH INTEREST RATES
3. LONG REPAYMENT PLANS

DTI = DEBT TO INCOME RATIO

DTI SHOULD BE LESS THAN

36%

OF YOUR TAKE HOME PAY

36%

THE "LONG" TERM REPAYMENT PERIOD IS WHAT MAKES SCHOOL DEBT DANGEROUS!

AVOID SCHOOL DEBT OR PAY IT DOWN AS SOON AS POSSIBLE!

11

Saving

"If you know how to spend less than you get,
you have the philosopher's stone."
—Benjamin Franklin

Good job! You've climbed the step of goal-setting, which motivated you to take the next step of creating income. You then
budgeted your income streams so that you can take the next step
to financial independence: Saving! Saving is the most important
step needed to control your destiny. You cannot afford not to save
money! This is not an exaggeration or hyperbole. You can create
an exceptional short-term, mid-term and long-term future if you
can get control of this portion of your financial life. This one item
is what separates having the life you choose and love versus having
an exhausting daily struggle to make financial ends meet while you
work at a job you despise.

Saving is entirely the point of working to create income, budgeting that income and then getting rid of your debt monster. You
climb all of the other stair steps just to complete this one vital step!
All the chapters that you read before this one were designed and

written to help you figure out how to get to the point where you can save money. If you are already saving, the information here will hopefully help you save even more. Without savings, you are highly susceptible to any unexpected financial bump in the road like an illness or an automobile accident that injures you. Any of these could devastate your finances for a lifetime. Once you start getting upside down financially (owing more than you can pay), it is difficult and time-consuming to become financially healthy again. It is much easier to not become debt-laden from the beginning.

As we covered in previous chapters, your income is not unlimited. Even if you want to work as long as you live, it is unlikely your current employer will want to keep you forever. Employers like to push older workers out at a certain age. After that occurs, it is difficult to find another job with comparable pay because you were likely at the top of the pay grade in your field. I bring this issue up again because it highlights the urgency of creating savings to become financially secure and successful in the present and for the future.

Since you have read this far, you know that you should be saving 20 percent of your take-home pay. Can you save that much? If not, you are pretty consistent with your peers. Most Americans savings' rates are nowhere near the 20 percent range. Americans are, however, beginning to catch on and are saving more money. The personal savings rate in September 2019, as reported by The Bureau of Economic Analysis/U.S. Department of Commerce, is 8.3 percent[1]. This is an increase from the savings rate in 2000, which was only 4.2 percent[2]. This is still not adequate.

According Visual Capital[3], although there appears to be an initial relationship between annual income and net worth, that relationship fades quickly in just a short time period[4]. Spending, saving and investing habits are more relevant to net worth than income. You should remember this point: your net worth (all your assets minus your liabilities) has more to do with your savings rate than how much money you make.

There are two common financial mistakes that derail most Americans from saving. The first and most serious financial mistake Americans make is procrastinating saving until they are in their 40s. Money you save early in your saving career earns the largest return (money for you) over time. Your earliest savings creates the largest gains because these monies earn compounding interest for the longest period of time. Procrastinating until you are in your 40s handicaps the amazing power of compound interest to work on your behalf. Waiting until your 40s also significantly increases the amount you must remove from the family budget to have any chance at all of creating wealth in the future.

You should not wait to begin saving. Savings can give you significant financial freedom and peace of mind very early in your career. With significant savings at your command, you can be fearless and aggressive at work because you know you are never stuck with any particular job or any particular boss. You can leave whenever you like! That reduces your overall job and life stress. Saving early in your working career allows you to create an emergency fund with enough cash to pay all your bills and provide you with a living allowance for a year—assuming you had no job.

Let's say you make $60,000 in take-home pay annually. Remember the 50/30/20 budget? That includes the 50 percent for Needs and the 30 percent for the Wants categories. You could probably reduce the total 80 percent (for Needs and Wants) to 70 percent and still be fine. That means $60,000 x .70 = $42,000 in an emergency fund if you make an average salary.

You should put most of your savings in an easily accessible, FDIC (Federal Deposit Insurance Corporation) or NCUA (National Credit Union Administration) insured money market fund, where banks or credit unions pay you a slightly higher interest than a savings account. You should also place $3,000 to $5,000 into an interest-bearing checking account so that you always have a cushion and quick access to a pile of cash capable of handling most emergencies. Be sure to shop around for the highest paying/ insured, interest bearing checking and money market accounts with the lowest fees.

A large amount of money kept for emergencies situations is called cash reserves or liquid reserves in the financial world. It is used to fund emergency expenses in your life for a limited period of time. Without an emergency fund, your debt reduction or savings plan can easily be derailed.

The second biggest mistake most people make is failing to increase their savings annually as they make more and more income over time. As they increase their income at work, the 20 percent should also increase. When I first started saving, I began with only $50 a month. That was far from the 20 percent I needed. I made up for that low amount as I saved more and more money over time. By the time I left the police department, my wife and I were saving half our combined take-home income. Saving half our income was not a hardship because we always budgeted. Before I left the department, our day-to-day Wants category (30 percent of one of our incomes) was much higher than most of my peers who now had minimal or nonexistent discretionary money. My peers were now mired in debt and had very little extra money. Remember, this group had already worked 20 to 30 years. What did they have to show for it?

We scrimped and struggled early, so it could count for a great deal later. My peers scrimped later, but were now being frugal only in an attempt to service their growing debt monsters. Many people are so mired in debt they can't manage to save a year's worth of expenses. What everyone can do is save $2,000 or $3,000 to use as a mini-emergency fund for the mishaps that inevitably arise. Then concentrate on your debt reduction plans. Without that cushion, any bump in the road will derail your debt pay-down plan.

Saving money requires self-discipline. It requires deferring spending today so you can enjoy an even bigger and better tomorrow. For so many people, self-discipline is in short supply. The seductive power of having what you want right now, by using credit or money you don't yet have, is very strong. There are several things you can do, however, that will help you stay on track with your savings plan. The first thing you can do is focus on your financial goals. Consider the benefits of achieving your goals by working through your action plans. Get excited about your goals and celebrate your progress toward achieving those goals. Distract yourself from spending by focusing on goal achievement.

The second thing you can do is automate your savings. If you have direct deposit, you can have the sum you designate routed to your savings account or investment accounts rather than going into your checking. That way you don't even see it or have to think about saving. Saving in this manner, along with automating your monthly bills reduces your stress. The strategy of automating whatever you can on your budget absolutely works and was one of the primary methods my wife and I used to build our wealth!

Finally, understand that the tasks of creating income, budgeting and saving will get easier as time passes. Remember, most of the angst and discomfort is temporary and will end if you stick with your program. If you give up and stop doing any real budgeting and saving, it will never end as there will never be enough money. Think about that for a minute. If you don't get your money and budget under control, you will always have low financial means for the rest of your life. I want more for you and sincerely hope you also want more for yourself.

My wife and I are moderately wealthy, yet we still budget each and every day. Neither of us just go out and buy random items. If we want something, we budget for it and wait until the money is available. Everyone who is financially successful does this. Some of our friends find it very odd that we still stick to a budget. They don't understand why I just don't buy whatever I want. I try to explain to these friends that both my wife and I spent years and years building this wealth. After all that time, energy and effort, you become protective of your money-producing nest egg. You are not just going to spend it on random Want items.

Savings are not just for retirement, although your savings will make retirement possible. Savings provide you with more financial freedom and an improved quality of life today, tomorrow and the next day. Saving is a key step in achieving control of your life and perhaps the most important stair step needed to build the future you are striving to obtain.

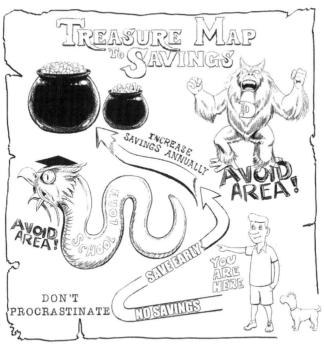

AUTOMATE SAVINGS
USE DIRECT DEPOSIT FROM PAYCHECK

CREATE AN EMERGENCY FUND OF AT LEAST
70% OF YOUR ANNUAL TAKE-HOME PAY!

12

Investing: The Life-changing Power of Opportunity Costs

"A pessimist sees the difficulty in every opportunity; an optimist sees the opportunity in every difficulty."
—Winston S. Churchill

Congratulations! You've done the hard work of settings goals, beaten back the debt monster, budgeted the income you've earned, and you're saving. You have earned the right to take the next stair step to your financial independence: investing. This section will teach proven and generally accepted investment principles and best portfolio management practices to minimize your investment risks while maximizing your returns. My personal experience in this area strongly suggests the principles I am going to explain to you are true and relevant.

My wife and I, and many others, have used these financial investing principles in our own lives. Be advised, however, I am not an investment advisor. I do not give investment advice. I am a Certified Financial Education Instructor with the National

Financial Educators Council[1]. I have extensive experience teaching financial principles to various groups, from jail inmates to doctors. I have considerable experience writing on personal finance subjects. My previous book, *Messages From Your Future: The Seven Rules for Financial, Personal and Professional Success*[2] advocated for achieving financial independence early in life. I explained in that book that your present actions travel outward through time and create your future—either a positive or negative one. This is also true with personal finances.

I'll explain investing concepts in very simple and concise terms. You should do absolutely nothing that I discuss, however, unless you independently research and verify the information I give you. In fact, this book should be the beginning of your education, not the end (see the suggested reading list at the end of the book). The same caution is warranted with any financial book or any financial information you read, no matter where it comes from. After research, always make your own independent decisions to keep you and your money safe. Understand that in both life and investing, there are never any guarantees.

If you did the exact same things I did, it might lead to very different results due to market and economic forces, future events and your ability to utilize the principles described in these pages. To earn your trust, I can tell you that I sell absolutely no investment products whatsoever. I have no financial interest in you purchasing any particular investment or investment product. In the spirit of full disclosure, I will say we own various index funds and a few random, individual stocks (as a very small portion of our overall portfolio) as well as bonds and certificates of deposit.

The majority of our population simply does not know most of the information you are going to read. An entire financial industry is devoted to making this information seem as complicated as possible. After all, if you feel you can't do it, then they get to do it for you— at a significant cost. Even if you finally decide to let someone else manage this for you, the next few chapters contain the information necessary to help you monitor what he or she is doing (or should be doing) with your investments.

Learning investing concepts has become urgent and vital. Our work worlds are changing. Retirement plans are phasing out defined benefit (DB) saving plans. These are plans where the employer creates a pension for you and manages the investments that fund the pension payments to its retirees[3]. Businesses absolutely detest these plans because it puts all the responsibility for a pension upon their shoulders. Instead, most companies (except for some government jobs) have moved to Defined Contribution (DC) plans that put the burden upon the employee to save and invest their own money.

The American public, however, has not caught up to this economic trend. According to The 2018 National Financial Capability Study, only 30 percent understand basic financial and investing principles required to make this type of system work for them[4]. We are going to begin to change that paradigm, starting now!

One of the most important investing concepts is the concept of opportunity costs. Understanding this concept can change your life for the better. You can use this concept for investing purposes and many other areas in your day-to-day living. The concept of opportunity cost (for investments) says that if you invest your money in one option, you automatically lose the opportunity and benefits of utilizing the next best option. What that means in the investing world is that you calculate the costs and benefits of two or three investing options and then make an informed decision based upon your particular needs.

Take investing in Certificates of Deposit, for example. CDs are an investment product issued by financial institutions such as banks, credit unions and brokerage companies that are similar to savings bonds. They are insured and an extremely safe investment. If you invest a $1,000 in a 12-month CD (using an interest rate of 2.5 percent as an example), you will earn $25 in profit at the end of the year ($1,000 x 1.025) with almost no risk. If you invest that same $1,000 in the stock market, however, you could earn six to 12 percent interest and that could potentially give you as much as $60 in profit. On the surface, it seems that you could make at least $35 more in one year by putting your $1,000 into a stock market investment—making the stock market your best option.

Not so fast, though. Let's consider your needs. When do you need your money? If you need it right away or fairly soon, the CD is tied up for one year. If you cash in the CD early, you take a big penalty, which will likely cause you to lose, not make, money. Perhaps buying the CD might not be a good choice.

When you use the stock market for investing, the longer your money is invested, the greater your chances of making a profit with stocks—particularly with index funds. In the short-term, however, you are just as likely to lose money as you are to make money. So, for a short-term investment, CDs are most likely not your best investment and the stock market is a good long-term investment, but not a great investment for less than five years.

Actually, if you needed the money back reasonably soon, you could use the money market account I mentioned previously that pays you interest as long as you maintain the pre-designated balance in your account (if your financial institution has such a requirement). Money can usually move in and out of such accounts without penalty—up to a certain number of monthly transactions.

The concept of opportunity cost is useful in other areas of your life as well. As an example, we can discuss one of my primary vices and the opportunity costs associated with this vice. I love diet cola from a popular, nationwide, fast-food chain. I drink their diet soda almost every day. Also, I don't have just one diet soda, but usually three a day. I already know that this habit is not healthy. Since I really like my vice, however, I'm willing to make sacrifices. Let's move on to analyzing my opportunity costs with these purchases:

Diet Soda: Cost = $1.50 per fountain soda

- 3 diet sodas = 3 x $1.50 = $4.50 daily
- $4.50 x 365 = $1,642.50 annually (plus wear and tear on vehicle and gas)

So now we all know (especially my lovely wife) that I spend $1,642.50 on diet soda annually. My next best alternative would be drinking diet soda by purchasing two-liter bottles and cans of diet soda. Spending less or reducing the costs of items you utilize regularly is called reducing your "costs per unit." Due to past experience, I already know my canned or two-liter soda costs work out to be $30 a month, assuming I bought no fountain soda. So, on the surface, I would save $1,282.50 annually, plus wear and tear on my car.

But, of course, that is not the end of it. Some would say the best alternative is not buying any diet soda because it's not good for me. Using the alternative of no diet soda, I could put $4.50 daily into a money market account. I would end up with a monthly deposit of approximately $136.88. If I put my $136.88 into a money market account each month for one year I would make approximately 2.5 to three percent interest. For this estimate, I used three percent. The deposits plus interest accrued work out to be $1,669.50, with a profit of $26.94 the first year (using an online compound interest calculator)[5]. So I would make $26.94, plus save the $1,642.50. I might also work out my transportation costs (there and back) if I wanted to analyze my savings further using IRS calculations per mile driven.

What does it look like if I drink no soda and save my money for five years? Using the compound interest calculator once more, I learn that I would have deposited $4,927.68 and made $234.70 in interest. This account would now hold a total of $5,162.38. The numbers keep getting larger as time passes. Analyzing opportunity costs and then selecting the best opportunity maximizes the money you can have now and can accumulate. A seemingly insignificant choice in life can actually appreciably impact your future.

Now let's consider a much more important example of the opportunity cost principle, which will really highlight how impactful this principle is in your everyday life. A couple years ago, I decided that I wanted a new Chevrolet Camaro. I have wanted one since I was kid. I reached a point where I felt we could easily afford this luxury. Of course, the car I was driving was paid off and ran great. There was absolutely no urgent need to get rid of it. However, I felt that I could easily afford to treat myself and purchase a Camaro. I went to my lovely wife and explained that I wanted to make this purchase. After discussing this for a short time, my wife said, "Well, think about it for a while, dear." In our shared/learned language from our time together, this meant the discussion was tabled for a while. That was totally fair and I had no problem with thinking a bit longer about this rather large purchase. Of course, my "thinking" about the purchase turned out to only be about how much I really wanted a new Camaro and not the opportunity costs of the purchase.

A couple weeks later, I approached my lovely wife again. I said, "I've thought a lot about the Camaro and I really want to buy one." My lovely wife looked up from her computer, smiled sweetly and said, "Sure, honey! Go ahead and research it and then get one if you want." Then she went back to her computer. Now you might think I was home free! Just find a car I like and buy it. Actually, she was three steps ahead of me, as she usually is, and had no worries I would actually spend our money on one.

What my wife had probably already researched, and now knew, was that the new Camaro model I wanted cost in the neighborhood of $55,000. Going to my loan calculator[6], I typed in $15,000 down on this purchase while financing the rest. I soon learned that car loans were running about six percent annually. I looked at a five-year loan at six percent with $15,000 down and financing $40,000 over five years. The results were very, very ugly.

New Car Purchase Analysis:

- Total price: $55,000
- Financed amount: $40,000
- Monthly payment: $773.31
- Total interest paid over five years: $6,398.
- The original $40,000 financed + $6,398 interest = $46,398
- Total $46,398 (+$15,000 down payment) = $61,398 (my total cost)

Shockingly, I realized that the purchase would not only deprive me of savings, but also the six percent income my money was creating for me in our investment portfolio over that same time period. If I just took the money out of our account and paid cash to avoid the interest charges, the math becomes even worse. I would have lost the opportunity to make a whopping

$19,186 to $35,491 in compounding interest income that our money was creating over the same five-year period (at six percent to 10 percent) if I simply left the $55,000 in the account. That information settled the issue. If someone was going to make that kind of money, I definitely wanted it to be me and not a finance company. Of course, my wife knew all of this already because she had no doubt completed this analysis long before we discussed it again. She knew there was no possible way I would lose both the purchase amount and the income this money could possibly generate to buy a new Camaro. Remember, I don't actually need a new Camaro and my cars ran just fine. Two years later, I am still driving the same car. It has 100,000 miles on it and still runs great; still no need to get rid of my old car.

The point of opportunity cost is that the purchase price of an item can be deceptive. Opportunity costs are always higher than the simple purchase price plus the interest payments. You are choosing not to save that money in a compound-interest generating account, which has a huge upside potential.

Remember, the entire point of budgeting and saving to create a nest egg is to use compounding interest to generate an independent income stream for your use forever. If you kill the nest egg by removing all or part of your monies from your investment accounts, it is not available to generate income for your use. So withdraw wisely from your nest egg and consider the long-term negative impact to determine if you should make a purchase.

OPPORTUNITY COSTS:

WHEN YOU CHOOSE ONE OPTION, YOU
LOSE THE OPPORTUNITIES & BENEFITS
OF THE OTHER CHOICES.

OPPORTUNITY COSTS OF NEW SPORTS CAR:

OPPORTUNITY COSTS CHOICES:

1. FINANCE CAR AT 6% INTEREST = $61,398

2. PAY CASH FOR SPORTS CAR = $55,000

3. LEAVE MONEY IN INVESTMENTS &
CREATE OPPORTUNITY TO MAKE FROM
6% TO 10% COMPOUNDING INTEREST
OVER 5 YEARS =

$19,000 TO $35,000

PURCHASE PRICE OF A CONSUMER ITEM CAN BE DECEPTIVE

COSTS ARE *ALWAYS* HIGHER
THAN SIMPLE PURCHASE PRICE
PLUS ANY INTEREST CHARGES

13

Investing: Time Value of Money and Compounding Interest

"The best time to plant a tree was twenty years ago.
The second best time is now."
—Chinese proverb

You are climbing a very tall mountain. The mountainside is rocky, steep and dangerous. You knock one rock loose. It is just a single stone. No problem! You watch it roll down the mountainside you just climbed. This rock collides with another rock and those two rocks, in turn, roll down the hill and begin colliding with two more rocks and so on. The number of rocks and their size keeps growing exponentially as the force builds during their tumble down the mountain. Once the rocks get close to the base of the mountain, they have become an unstoppable avalanche that will crush anyone or anything that stands in their thundering path! This is the incredible power of compounding interest.

Here is what happens in compounding interest: You invest your money and when you are paid interest on your account balance, the balance becomes larger. Your balance now includes your original investment and the interest you were just paid on your investment for a month (or whatever interest accruing period is designated). The next month, you get interest on this larger balance and so on. If you do nothing and leave it alone, it gets larger and larger (continues to compound) until it becomes a massive force in the future. This is how you will convert a one-time investment of $1,000 for 30 years at 10 percent into almost $20,000 in your future. Just to make a quick comparison, if you only obtained "simple interest" (no compounding) on $1,000 over the same time period and at the same interest rate, you would only have a meager $4,000 in your account after 30 years. In other words, each month you are only paid interest on your original $1,000. This allows you to see how powerful compounding interest can be.

You can gain control of this dollar avalanche and make it work to your benefit or you can stand at the bottom of the mountain and watch your impending destruction barrel down the mountainside toward you at increasing speed and power. By borrowing large amounts of money or by letting the balance of many small loans get large, you give the keys of your destruction to others and allow this incredible power to be utilized against you. Like in the ancient days of the Greek and the Roman empires, you willingly submit to the slavery of debt. This is not an exaggeration. Many, many people owe so much money they can't pay the interest payments on their loans. According to creditcard.com[1], 65 percent of people believe they will never be able to get out of debt in their lifetime[2].

In investing, the elements of compounding interest include your principal (amount you originally invest), the interest rate (the rate of return you will receive on your investment) and the amount of time your investments have to work for you. The final element is the number of times it will compound during the time your money is invested. Just to be thorough, here is the formula for compounding interest (deep breath—you really don't have to know this):

A = P(1 + r/n)

- A = total value
- P = the original amount deposited in the account to gain interest
- r = the interest rate
- n = the number of times it compounds during the accruing period (daily, monthly, quarterly or yearly)
- t = time period the interest will accrue

I could work through this formula, but I have never found any reason to do so. Instead, I go to one of the many online compound calculators. The Calculator Site[3] has an array of financial calculators. It provides you the final answer in a nice spreadsheet format that includes a breakdown of all the elements for each compounding period. There are also plenty of free apps for your smartphone that will do this job for you.

The Rule of 72 is a quick rule of thumb that I enjoy using to estimate how long it will take my money to double. If you earn six percent on your investment, this rule states you should divide 72 by six (percent). This simple equation would look like this:

72 / 6(%) = 12 years

Therefore, you know it would take roughly 12 years to double your money at six percent interest. The larger the interest rate, the less accurate this rule of thumb becomes. This is a general idea and is not a hard and fast calculation.

The more often your investment compounds, the (slightly) more money you make. In other words, if your investment compounds at an annual six percent and it compounds daily, it is slightly more than if your investment compounds monthly. Quarterly compounding, of course, creates slightly more money than compounding annually. Below is a basic example of how often various compounding periods impact your money:

- $1,000 earning 6% annually compounded daily for 5 years = $1,349.83
- $1,000 earning 6% annually compounded monthly for 5 years = $1,348.85
- $1,000 earning 6% annually compounded quarterly for 5 years = $1,346.86
- $1,000 earning 6% annually compounded annually for 5 years = $1,338,23

There is just under a $10 difference (approximately) between compounding daily and annually over a five-year period. Of course, you can easily flip this entire concept and make it work against you with your use of debt and loans. Below are the most common loan types and how often they typically compound:

- Student loans are compounded daily.
- Credit cards are compounded daily.
- Mortgages are compounded on the balance and are based on an amortization table—a schedule of payments that are weighted heavily toward paying the interest before the principal (original purchase price) balance is paid down.
- Car loans are also an amortized schedule with interest payments being paid/loaded up-front or paid first.

Compounding interest also closely supports the concept of the time value of money. The time value of money (TVM) dictates that money today is better than that same amount sometime in the future. The reasons include the inflation rate and compounding interest. Inflation means that if you hide $100,000 under your mattress for a decade, it is worth significantly less when you drag it out 10 years later. The inflation rate is the rise in costs of goods and services in our economy from one year to the next. Usually, but not always, goods you purchase and the services you consume go up in price as time passes. The amount by which these goods and services go up is calculated by the government (Bureau of Labor Statistics) and is reported as a percentage, called the inflation rate.

Some examples of how goods rise in cost over time:

- 1970: average new car cost $3,542[4]
- 1990: average car cost $9,437[5]
- 2000: average new car cost $15,357[6]
- 2019: average new car cost $35,742[7]

The inflation rate, as of November of 2019, is considered to be 1.7 percent annually[8]. That means almost everything (depending on production levels) costs 1.7 percent more today than it did last year.

The three investing concepts of opportunity costs, time value of money (TVM) and compound interest are concepts everyone needs to know to be successful. All of these concepts are also extremely relevant to our day-to-day personal finance decisions. These ideas work in unison to create financial prosperity—or to create financial scarcity. The opportunity costs of using a dollar include losing the ability of that dollar to produce more dollars or income on your behalf.

The TVM states that the sooner you can invest that dollar, the more time it has to create more dollars for your benefit. This concept is also closely related to the term Present Discounted Value (PDV), or how much you are willing to pay today to receive more money or additional income payments on this money in the future. These terms all support the concept that the money you invest first grows the most. Begin investing early!

These concepts are true whether you know it or not or whether you even acknowledge they exist. Every dollar we earn has both a potential and a consequence. Your decision to use a dollar to create wealth or to spend it on consumer items go well beyond simply spending or saving dollars in your household budget. Remember, your lifetime earnings are not infinite and you have a limited number of dollars coming your way. Each dollar you save can create even more dollars for your use later. Those dollars then create even more dollars for you, and so on until the avalanche happens!

1 ROCK = $1 **COMPOUNDING INTEREST ELEMENTS**

1. PRINCIPLE (AMOUNT INVESTED)
2. TIME
3. INTEREST RATE
4. WHEN INTEREST RATE COMPOUNDS
   -DAILY
   -MONTHLY
   -QUARTERLY
   -ANNUALLY

FINANCIAL INDEPENDENCE EXPLOSION

$1
$2
$4
$8
$16
$32
$64

TIME

YOU WILL OBTAIN A LIMITED AMOUNT OF WAGES IN YOUR LIFETIME!

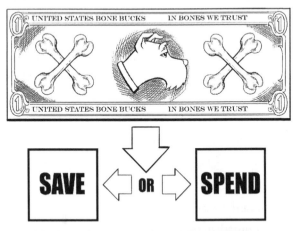

YOUR DECISION TO SAVE OR SPEND IS MORE IMPORTANT THAN STAYING WITHIN A HOUSEHOLD BUDGET!

EVERY DOLLAR YOUR SPEND IS NOT AVAILABLE TO MAKE NEW DOLLARS FOR YOU!

14

Investing: Investment Vehicles

"The person who says it cannot be done should not
interrupt the person who is doing it."
—Chinese proverb

Section One

For Everyone

Building financial independence in your day-to-day life will require you to have a variety of tools at your disposal. The tools in this case are composed of different financial checking, savings and investing accounts that all serve slightly different purposes. Some tools will provide you with cash immediately, while others are long-term investing accounts. Although this may seem complicated at first glance, I assure you it is not. Stay with this narrative and you will be rewarded with more knowledge than most people possess on this subject.

The method I teach begins by funding an interest-bearing checking account that can be obtained at a financial institution such as a credit union or bank. Our family's strong preference is a credit union for lower fees and higher customer satisfaction across the financial services spectrum. As a credit union member, you usually receive better terms on a wide range of financial products and accounts. In interest-bearing checking accounts, routine account fees are waived and interest is paid monthly on your balance. In some of these accounts, free checks are provided.

Some interest-bearing checking accounts require you to maintain a balance, while others do not. Shop around for the best rates and lowest fees. Keeping a small reserve in your checking account is never a bad idea as it will help eliminate accidental overdrafts and other types of punitive fees. The purpose of an interest-bearing checking account is to eliminate checking account fees, save money on checks and earn interest on the checking account balance rather than suffer a monthly fee to use a checking account.

After your checking account, you will also need a savings account that is linked to your checking. Using a linked savings account will help you smooth out minor problems and minor emergencies when they inevitably occur. The savings account is not permission to bust your budget. You will simply have these accounts, with a positive balance, to handle day-to-day issues that inevitably arise.

The next tool in your toolbox is a high-interest, money market savings account. You utilize this account to store your long-term emergency savings. This is where you keep your years' worth of savings to cover bills and expenses for an emergency situation. As of this writing, these accounts are paying just under three percent. Money market accounts limit the number of monthly transactions on the account. This is not a good account for money that must flow in and out on a regular basis. For money that flows in and out regularly, use your checking or your savings accounts to minimize the risk of a possible overdraft.

Your money market account at your bank should be insured either by the Federal Deposit Insurance Corporation (FDIC) or the National Credit Union Administration (NCUA) for credit unions. If your money market savings account is at the same financial institution as your checking account and your savings account, you can probably link them all together.

Another investing vehicle is your company-sponsored 401(k) (a 457 if you are a government employee or 403B if you are a non-profit employee). I will use "401(k)" through the rest of the book to include the 403B and 457 accounts since they are very similar. A 401(k) is a tax-deferred account, meaning the money is deposited into this account and grows without tax liability until you begin to withdraw money from it after age 59 1/2 (for 457 accounts, withdrawals can be made at age of retirement, even if that age is before 59 1/2.). When you withdraw money from this account, you pay the regular income tax rate based on your current applicable federal, state and local income tax bracket.

Employers ordinarily will match the money you contribute to your 401(k)—up to a certain percentage of your pay. Learn from your employer, by contacting human resources/benefits, to find out what percentage of your pay your company will match. Be sure to contribute enough to obtain your employer's full match. Otherwise, you are passing up your employer's money that can boost your investing and savings plan. Not taking steps to obtain this money creates a huge opportunity cost for you and is damaging to your future. All the tax rules governing 401(k)-type accounts can be found on the government IRS site[1]. Many company-sponsored plans are fee-heavy (see fee section), including the dreaded expense called "revenue sharing." Revenue sharing is a bonus paid by the 401(k) management firm to your employer to attract them as a customer. This actually means the 401(k) management company is giving kickbacks to "record keepers" (most likely your employer). Yes, this is legal, but in my view not ethical unless this information is stated clearly upfront.

Some employee-based 401(k) management firms only provide employees with a very limited selection of investment funds and at higher "retail prices" than the discounted institutional prices, which should be provided to company employees. Recent successful lawsuits, however, have knocked these two practices back on their heels, and they are now becoming less and less common.

Sadly, most of your employer's supervisory administration has no idea what fees your 401(k) charges you. Even worse, very few of them actually know what they are being charged to use their own company's 401(k) plan. No one, except for the HR benefits employee who handles your company's 401(k) benefit plan is likely to know the fee information—if they even know.

Luckily, over the last few years, most employers now offer better funds with much lower fees and no revenue sharing. Fee descriptions are also contained in the lengthy, legally worded prospectus—a document that describes your 401(k) plan. If you have the patience, you can eventually ferret out the fees you are charged. One of my wife's prior employers used a company to manage her 403B. This 401(k) management company charged an additional one percent on all her money. She read through over 100 pages of the prospectus to find the fee buried deep in the text.

Your strategy, assuming your employer's 401(k) charges many fees, is to contribute just enough to obtain your employer's maximum match. You are willing to put up with higher fees in this instance because the matching funds contributed by your employer provide such an overwhelming benefit to your bottom line that it overcomes this deficit. There are few other investments

where you are guaranteed to double your money almost immediately after the deposit. Take full advantage of your employer's
401(k) up to their matching limit.

If your 401(k) is not fee-heavy and you have good choices
(diversity and index funds—see portfolio in Chapter 19), the
current IRS rules allow you to contribute up to $19,000 annu-
ally; if you are over 50 years of age, you can contribute $24,000
annually with additional catch-up options.

After you have an emergency fund in a high interest-bearing money market account and you get all the available matching
funds provided by your employer's 401(k), then you can move
on to the next phase of saving and investing—an individual retirement account (IRA). The traditional IRA has similar rules to
your employer's 401(k). Your investment is tax-free until you make
withdrawals at age 59 1/2 . You are allowed to invest up to $6,000
pre-taxed annually—or up to $7,000 annually if you are over 50
years of age. How much you contribute to a personal IRA is not
impacted by you or your employer's contribution to your company's 401(k). If you make over $189,000, however, your eligibility
begins to be limited and is then eliminated altogether. Check the
IRS site for the latest rules[2].

Another option is a type of IRA known as a Roth IRA, which
is an account funded with income you have already paid taxes on.
A Roth IRA grows entirely tax-free. Your withdrawals, after age 59
1/2 are also entirely tax-free. You can withdraw your initial contributions to your Roth (that you have already paid taxes on) at any
time with no tax or penalties. However, you may not withdraw
the earnings in your Roth before age 59 1/2 without significant
penalties. Roth IRA rules dictate that you must make less than
$120,000 annually or $189,000 if filling jointly. After that income

level, your allowable contributions are restricted and then eliminated if you make more money. The tax code currently allows you to contribute to either a traditional IRA or a Roth IRA account. You could do both, but the total amount you are permitted to invest into these accounts remains $6,000 (or $7,000 if over 50 years old). As stated earlier, your employer's 401(k) does not impact the $6,000 total. Choosing a traditional IRA, a Roth IRA or a combination of both depends on whether you need a tax break now or in the future.

The biggest advantages of opening an IRA account, traditional or Roth, is that you choose which company you use. The company you choose will typically grant you access to hundreds if not thousands of funds (at cheaper rates) to maximize your investment diversification, meaning many different and unrelated investments. When the company works for you, then you can assure you receive fair treatment regarding fees. Large brokerages firms like Fidelity, Vanguard and E*TRADE offer IRAs (these are only examples and are not meant as recommendations). To discourage you from withdrawing your money from your tax deferred retirement accounts earlier than 59 1/2, significant penalties, including a 10 percent penalty after all regular taxes, will be assessed. Removing money from these accounts early creates huge opportunity costs that could derail your goals and future financial independence.

Are you confused? I certainly hope not. Here is a summary just in case. Use various interest-bearing accounts for different purposes. Your first priority is to open an interest-bearing checking account to avoid fees, avoid paying for checks and earn monthly interest payments on the money in your checking account. Then you follow with a savings account to help smooth out the routine rough spots you encounter with your budget. You then place your emergency fund (containing at least 70 percent of your annual salary) into a money market account to gain higher interest payments on this money.

The next priority is to secure your employer's 401(k) matching funds if available. Sometimes, your company 401(k) investment plans are laden with high fees. If your 401(k) has high fees, only deposit enough money in your company's 401(k) to obtain all matching funds. The last step is to fund a traditional IRA and/or a Roth account (Roth with after-tax money) to allow you to do tax planning in the future. This strategy will allow you to control your income tax liability in the future and allow you room for proactive tax planning with your tax professional.

Section Two

For Independent Contractors and Small Business Owners

If you are an independent contractor or a small business owner, the information in this chapter is vital to your future. I recommend you create the same bank accounts as listed above until you get to the long-term savings and investing accounts. The IRS has created special accounts for independent contractors and small business owners. The best part is, you get to choose a brokerage company that has low fee options—like Fidelity or Vanguard. Additionally, you get elevated limits on how much you can invest in these various tax-deferred accounts.

The first option for the small business owner is a long-term plan called a Savings Incentive Match Plan For Employees (SIMPLE IRA). This works similarly to a traditional IRA. As a small business owner, you can contribute up $12,000 or up to $14,500 if you are 50 years old or older in pre-tax income. If you have a small business with employees, however, this plan requires you to set up accounts for them and provide some matching funds for their accounts as well.

The next option is the Simplified Employee Pension Plan (SEP-IRA). You can save up to 25 percent of your pay in pre-tax dollars up to $53,000 annually. If you have employees, you are required to contribute to their accounts as much as you contribute to your own.

The next tool for a small business owner or independent contractor is the solo or one-participant 401(k). This is for a business that has no employees such as an independent contractor. You can even start one of these accounts for both you and your spouse. This plan's big advantage is that you can save the first $19,000 you earn tax-free. If you are over 50, you can save the first $25,000 you make completely tax-free, until you make withdrawals after age 59 1/2. That is not all. Your business can contribute "profit sharing" contributions into your solo 401(k) account up to 25 percent of your pay to a maximum of $53,000 or $59,000 if you are over 50. You can also borrow on the balance of this account for short-term loans. You pay the loan back to yourself with interest.

Small business owners and self-employed contractors should begin saving and start one of these accounts as soon as they have an emergency fund. You can set up and contribute to these accounts and take full advantage of the power of the compounding interest to create wealth in your future. If you can create these kinds of financial resources, you will get the opportunity to decide what kind of future you will have! If not, you must take whatever you end up with at the end of your working career.

Even though I have talked about using retirement accounts as your primary investment vehicles, I am still loyal to my stated intent for writing this book. If you have followed my recommendations, you have created an adequate emergency fund, reduced your debt, automated most parts of your budget, and utilized 401(k), traditional, and/or Roth IRA investment vehicles. Remember, Roth IRAs allow you to remove the dollars you invested at any time. Although I don't recommend taking that action, you certainly could if a catastrophic event like a serious illness occurred.

Section Three
Investments Outside the Tax Deferment Structure

I usually avoid investing outside the tax-deferred retirement account structure because the impact of our tax system on investments made outside of these various tax-sheltered saving structures. Our tax system adds a whole tier of tax liability to any profits you might make on investments outside the deferred retirement systems. Essentially, you would have to deal with a whole new fee structure, and make no mistake, it is complicated. I strongly recommend a tax professional and an investment professional to guide and advise you if this is the path you choose. Below is a very simplified overview of the taxes you can expect to pay on investment profits outside tax-sheltered accounts:

15% on dividend earnings

35% on any investment profits you sell if you have owned them a year or less

15% on profits if you have owned the investments longer than one year

Interest (investment income) depends on your normal tax rate or marginal rate

Essentially, you pay taxes on all capital gains. Capital gains are the profits you make when you sell your investment(s). Many of the tax rates on capital gains also vary depending upon your current income bracket. Please note that a tax professional and an investment professional also adds another cost or fee structure to your investment outside the tax deferment structures. For the average wage-earner, investing outside the IRS tax deferred structure is very complicated and is a method I do not teach.

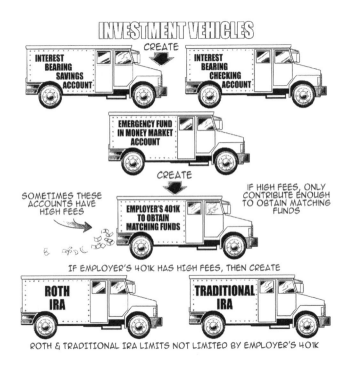

SELF EMPLOYED
TAX-DEFERRED PLANS

SOLO IRA
-NO EMPLOYEES
-UP TO $19,000
- CAN OPEN ONE FOR
YOUR SPOUSE
- CAN PROFIT
SHARE FROM YOUR
BUSINESS UP TO 25%
OR $53,000

SIMPLE IRA
-UP TO $12,000
ANNUALLY
-MUST PROVIDE
MATCHING TO
EMPLOYEES

SEP IRA
-UP TO 25% ANNUALLY OR
$53,000 IN PROFIT SHARING
-MUST PROVIDE MATCHING
TO EMPLOYEES

15

Investing: Fees and Indexed Mutual Funds

"Experience is a good school. But the fees are high."
—Heinrich Heine

Gazelles are the animal kingdom's version of fast-food on the African Savannah. Their nickname is "McDonalds" because of the black, M-shaped marking on the back of their rumps and because all predators will gladly eat gazelles. Even smaller predators and omnivores, like eagles and baboons will eat young gazelles if they can catch them. This grazing animal supports an entire ecosystem of predators in the biodiverse African grasslands. You and your money play the role of the gazelle in the retail financial investment world. An entire financial services ecosystem feeds off of you and your money. Wall Street does everything in its power to suck as many fees out of your herd as possible. Whether you know it or not, you are in a struggle over who ultimately gets possession of the dollars you invest. Wall Street uses various strategies to hunt and capture your herd.

The first strategy is the friendly local investment advisor. Financial advisors are usually paid via the sales commissions and other fees charged by the various stocks, bonds and mutual funds. When you invest in stocks, some funds pay the advisor a commission through the fees they collect from you. Sales commissions are commonly divided into two categories: front-load and back-load fees. Front loads are the percentage of your money you pay to buy into a fund that is kicked back to the salesman. Back loads are the percentage of your money that you pay the salesman when you withdraw your money from the fund, which is even more insidious.

The second strategy financial advisors employ against you is a legal document called the prospectus. This is a legalese document they seem to take pleasure in making as difficult as possible to read, sometimes hundreds of pages in length, and filled with very small print. In this document, they hide the fees that you are paying. If you read through every sentence, page and paragraph you can probably find all of the fees listed, unless you've blinked. My very smart wife, who has the patience and drive for this, will read the prospectus line by line and highlight all the fees she finds. Finding the fees in a prospectus is difficult because they obviously don't want you to notice or locate their hidden, money-sucking fees.

Most funds would much rather keep you in the dark regarding fees. Recently, there was a push by Congress to force funds to list all their fees on the first page and first section of the prospectus. The financial industry soon lobbied that crazy idea right out of existence. Now a new fiduciary rule is scheduled to take effect. The new rule dictates the investment advisor working with your retirement accounts (retirement accounts only) has the duty and legal obligation to act in your best interest (definition of a fiduciary). I remain extremely skeptical that will actually occur. After all, if they did follow this rule they would recommend nothing but very low-fee, index mutual funds. Index mutual funds traditionally have the lowest fees in the entire financial fund industry.

Fees hidden in the prospectus include the many sales commission fees that are described above, plus plenty of others. Those fees might include short-term trading fees that the mutual fund will charge should you sell your new fund within 90 days of purchasing it. This is to discourage you from day trading (trading in and out of funds daily, trying to make a quick profit). You may pay a fee called a 12(b)1 fee, which is an advertising fee charged when you withdraw your money from a mutual fund. This fee is usually paid to the nice salesman that put you in the fund.

The last fee I will discuss is the expense ratio. This is how much the mutual fund will charge you annually to manage the fund. This charge is legitimate, but it is only valid to a certain point. If this fee is too high, it will kill or significantly retard your growth of profits or hit you even harder when your fund has already been pushed down during a market dip. Index mutual funds charge nothing (if you are already a customer of certain brokerage houses) to as much as one percent, but most charge .02 to around .05 percent.

Actively managed funds (where an advisor is involved in actively buying and selling investments while trying to make a profit) can charge anywhere from one to over two percent on average. An actively managed fund includes even more expenses, such as brokerage fees that are charged for every purchase or sale of stocks within the fund. Also, fees are needed to pay the army of stock analysts who are searching for stocks that represent a good buy to attempt to beat market averages (averages as reflected by the various market sector indexes).

The fees don't seem very high at first glance, so let's do some basic math to show how fees can really impact you. Say, for example, a fund charges an expense ratio of one percent. That doesn't seem like much, but $100,000 x 1% = $1,000 charge on your investments. If your fund goes up in a given year, they take the new, higher amount and charge you the same one percent. So if you made only three percent during a slow year, after administrative fees, your fund is knocked down significantly because they still charge you a full one percent of your total, not just your profit. If you have more money, it just gets progressively worse. The seemingly meager one percent fee on $500,000 is now $5,000 annually, whether you make a dime or not. Fees are a very serious matter for informed investors and are one of several factors that make the difference between investing profitably or creating an investment flop. Financially Simple says that just 0.75 percent in investment fund management fees creates a 20 percent smaller nest egg over 20 years[1].

In an investor bulletin (No. 164)[2] noted a portfolio grown from scratch that now has a balance of $220,000, created over a 20-year period, making a steady four percent interest with a .50 percent annual administrative fee, has paid portfolio fund managers somewhere around $10,000 in annual payments over the 20 years. For the same period, with the same total amount, same interest rate and an administrative fee bumped up to a one percent ongoing annual fee, it will cost investors $30,000 over this same time period—which equals 14 percent of the total.

If using an advisor is the difference between you regularly investing your savings and not investing, then by all means use a financial advisor. The information in this book will at least help you understand what he or she is doing and the strategy he or she is utilizing. When I ask some people what their advisor is doing, they sometimes say, "I don't know, she (advisor) handles it." She might be handling it, but you get the result—or lack of result from her work. Know what your advisor is doing and their reasoning behind what they doing. Always discuss fees with your advisor and ask (never hurts) for lower fee investments.

Fees always matter, and they add up! Look to keep your fees low. Keep your gazelle dollars running through your own grassland to create more "little gazelle" dollars. Don't let the Wall Street predators run them down and eat them. Every dollar predators capture is one less dollar to grow exponentially in your compounding avalanche. Fees can be easily avoided, so it would be a shame to allow them to create a huge opportunity cost over time.

FEES ALWAYS MATTER! KEEP YOUR FEES LOW!

BACK LOAD FEE WHEN YOU WITHDRAW FROM FUNDS

YOUR MONEY

12(B)1 FEE

FRONT LOAD FEE WHEN YOU BUY FUND

EXPENSE RATIO FEE

YOUR MONEY SUPPORTS AN ENTIRE ECOSYSTEM OF WALL STREET FINANCIAL SERVICES VIA FEES TAKEN FROM YOU

KEEP FEES LOW!

.75% FEE = 20% SMALLER OVER 20 YEARS

$200,000 NEST EGG

16

Investing: Risk

"The person who does nothing does nothing."
—Anonymous

You invest to make a profit, of course. This is also called your "return on investment." An investment is something you purchase with the goal of creating a profit from it in the future. If you buy a consumer item (such as a car) it will not increase in value. Consequently, any consumer items, including most memorabilia, collectibles, or most precious metal products are not very good investments[1]. A profit on your investment occurs when your investment increases in price or when your investment creates a profit payment to you. You buy investments because you believe they will be worth more in the future or will provide you with income over time (like bonds). If an investment does not provide an income or increase in value, it is not a successful investment. Increasing your investment's value over time is considered successful investing and is the goal of this entire undertaking.

One of the best ways to learn about investing is discussing the concept of investing risk. Luckily, this essential concept is not at all difficult to comprehend! You could certainly make risk (in the area of investing) very complicated, but there is little reason to do so.

Investment returns are hugely impacted by the amount of risk you take when you decide to purchase an investment. For example, higher-risk classes of investments have the opportunity to create greater profits and greater returns on your principal (money you initially invested). When you invest in higher-risk investments, however, you could potentially make no profit or you could even lose your principal. The chance of making a larger profit is your additional compensation for putting your money at risk in a less secure investment[2]. Conversely, lower-risk investments produce lower returns because the risk of losing your money is much less and your chances of making a profit are almost assured.

The two most common types (classes) of investments are equities (stocks that are certificates of ownership of companies and corporations) and bonds (you loan your savings to the bond issuer who pays you your money back plus interest). Stocks are purchased with the hope that the company will become more valuable by making a profit and thereby make the company's stocks more valuable. Some larger companies pay shareholders (or stockholders) dividends (payments of their profit to stockholders). This can be conceptualized as profit-sharing payments to company owners. Owning part of a company (stockholder) is considered a higher risk because companies frequently suffer quarterly profit loses, fail to keep up with changing market conditions or go bankrupt for a variety of economic or internal issues. The additional risk inherent in company ownership is why stocks usually produce higher returns than bonds.

The higher return of stocks over safer investments, like bonds, is called the risk premium and is your compensation for investing your money in a more uncertain investment. Bonds are purchased so that you can receive interest payments in exchange for lending your money to the bond issuer and are generally considered much lower risk than stocks. Since bonds generally represent less of a financial risk, they tend to produce a lower return on your investment.

Both bonds and stocks come in different categories and sub-categories. Each category of stocks and bond has its own risk level. The higher the risk level, the greater the chance (not a guarantee) for a larger return (profit) on your investment. Your goal is to always get the best return on your investments at the lowest possible risk to your principal and at the lowest price (lowest fees).

Risk creates wide swings in investment prices called volatility. Volatility is measured and then calculated on the standard deviation of the stock price's travel range—both up and down[3]. If you didn't quite follow that, I understand. Try this explanation: it is not the statistical average of the stock prices, but the average range of the investment's price swing (both up and down) over time. A low standard deviation implies the price is more consistently valued and the number will be small. A high standard of deviation implies the price varies wildly and is represented by a higher number. Your takeaway is that riskier investments typically produce wider swings in price on a daily, monthly, quarterly and annual basis. These swings are called volatility. Risk and volatility work in tandem. Risk is totally subjective and is based entirely upon your opinion of the risk involved in purchasing any particular investment. Volatility, on the other hand, can be measured and easily tracked.

I'm going to mention a few more technical terms. Non-systematic risk, unsystematic risk, specific risk or diversifiable risk all mean the same thing—the risk an investor takes when he or she buys a specific company. Nonsystematic risk could also apply to a specific industry like auto manufacturing. A quick example of nonsystematic risk is if a company CEO is discovered to have embezzled money or when some other random problem with a company's banking occurs. The risk is limited to that company, not the whole industry (or "system"). Nonsystematic risk in an industry would be, for example, if people stopped buying cars and took public transportation. Nonsystematic risk can be reduced by holding a broad range of diverse investments (many different stocks in many different industries). Any specific company loss is offset by all the other companies you own.

Systematic risk is the very real risk that our economy could face a downturn or some other economic factor that will push your investments lower. With a downturn, it is not a question of "if" it happens but "when" and how long the downturn will last. This could be caused by a large increase in the inflation rate, an interest rate hike or some international event like a trade war. You can reduce this type of risk, at least somewhat, by the use of asset allocation or the mix of investment classes you own (like stocks versus bonds) in your portfolio.

You also need to know that riskier investments swing in value, sometimes significantly. However, these swings in prices actually drag down or retard the growth of your investments. This phenomena is called risk drag or volatility drag. Volatility drag slows your wealth creation. For example, if you own Company A, a 10 percent decline on $1,000 worth of Company A's stock will leave you with $900. The very next day, if Company A's stock price goes back up that same 10 percent, the actual rise is calculated only on the $900 you have left. To clarify, a 10 percent rise on $900 will only bring you back up to $990—not the $1,000 you initially possessed. Even an 11 percent rise on $900 will only return you to $999. To get your initial investment back, your stock would have to go higher than 11 percent in value.

Volatility drag becomes more apparent with a larger percentage swing. If you lose 30 percent of an investment's value on a bad day, you need the price to go back up 43 percent the next day to obtain the same amount you possessed before the stock dipped in price. Like compounding interest, these numbers quickly magnify if you have larger amounts, longer time periods or increased volatility.

You can easily see how volatility drag will hamper your forward progress. With every small downturn, your stocks shed value. When you consider the concept of opportunity costs, these losses become even more harmful to your bottom line. You lost money when you had an opportunity to buy a different investment (like a bond) that might have made a profit instead.

Naturally, volatility drag can be somewhat mitigated by owning a mix of investments. A broad mix of investments will typically stop your overall bottom line from dropping or at least greatly slow the drop, like a parachute. As some of your investments go down, others will rise in value. The rise of other investments will typically offset your loss. That way, the total money you have invested continues to rise, even if portions of your individual investments do not do well.

I will show you how to refine this concept in the asset allocation chapter (Chapter 19). Over the long haul, stocks historically return from six percent to up to 12 percent. Within a short time (meaning within two or three years), no one can say with any kind of certainty what stock prices will do. This means you must have a longer-term investment horizon (the point in time when you require the money) for stocks and other riskier investments.

From the explanation of risk and volatility, you can begin to see how important it is to understand basic investing principles. If you don't have a solid understanding of basic investing, you are going to waste a lot of time, money and effort trying to grow your money. Investing principles are not complicated or hard for you to understand, however. Keep reading to learn even more valuable investing principles.

RISK= GREATER CHANCE OF MAKING A LARGE PROFIT. ALSO, A GREATER CHANCE OF LOSING INVESTMENT OR NOT MAKING A PROFIT

RISK IS SUBJECTIVE!

LARGE RISK

RISK CREATES VOLATILITY.

VOLATILITY = LARGE SWINGS IN PRICE.

VOLATILITY

STOCK "A" PRICE

STOCKS ARE MUCH MORE VOLATILE THAN BONDS!

STOCKS = COMPANY OWNERSHIP.

AND COMPANIES HAVE BAD QUARTERS OR YEARS WHERE PROFITS ARE LOW.

VOLATILITY DRAG!

VOLATILITY DRAG RETARDS THE GROWTH OF YOUR NESTEGG.

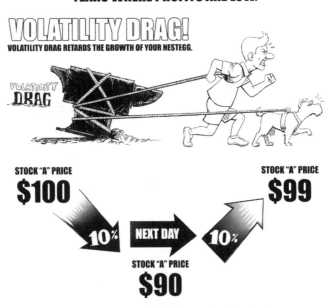

VOLATILITY DRAG

STOCK "A" PRICE
$100

10%   **NEXT DAY**   10%

STOCK "A" PRICE
$99

STOCK "A" PRICE
$90

IF ON A BAD DAY STOCK "A" GOES DOWN 25%, STOCK "A" WILL THEN HAVE TO GO UP 34% JUST TO GET EVEN!

17

Investing: The Short-term Direction of the Stock Market

"The best way to predict the future is to create it."
—Abraham Lincoln

In the world of investing, knowledge makes you strong! A lack of knowledge, conversely, makes you weak and allows others to easily take advantage of you. For example, you will frequently be told that a particular investment advisor knows where the stock market is headed. If you read or hear such a story on television, always view it with extreme skepticism. At this point in history, no one knows the short-term direction of the stock market or even the direction our broader financial markets are headed in the short term. What follows is a very brief history of economic research and explains why it is impossible to predict the short-term direction of the stock market, despite an army of Wall Street advisors ready to convince you otherwise. Of course, they likely want you to buy their investment picks (with fees kicked back to them) to offset the anticipated market downturn or maximize the anticipated market uptick.

Our investing system began with a crude financial market back in the 1300s when the Venetian traders traded private and public debt between themselves. This progressed to crude Belgium financial debt exchanges in 1500s. The first real stock exchange began in London, England. In America, the New York Stock Exchange was officially founded on May 17, 1792, under a Buttonwood tree on Wall Street[1] where stocks and other debt securities were traded back and forth between buyers and sellers. People have been trying to predict the stock market's short-term direction ever since.

In the early 1900s, Louis Bachelier devised his groundbreaking theory, "The Theory of Speculation," in which he stated that the price of a stock has nothing to do with a stock's historical price range movement and speculation (predicting a future price) based on the stock's historical price movements will not be accurate. Therefore, successful speculation (predicting future/higher or lower prices) on stock(s) in the short term is not possible[2]. This theory flies squarely in the face of so many people who say they can predict a stock's price direction by studying its history.

Francis Galton, in 1907, devised the next groundbreaking theory called, the "Wisdom of the Crowds." Galton went to numerous livestock auctions and would ask the crowd to guess the weight of a random steer in the pen. The crowd was usually successful and was typically off the actual confirmed weight by only a pound[3]. The practical application of this information to investing is that the crowd of investors who are buying and selling stocks or securities has accurately predicted the worth, value and correct price of stocks and other securities they are buying and selling. Therefore, at any particular moment in time, the price at which the stock is selling is, in fact, the correct price.

In 1990, Harry Markowitz won the Nobel Prize for Modern Portfolio Theory (MPT), which was a truly groundbreaking concept that he constructed in 1952. In this theory, one can obtain optimal returns by holding a mix of investment types (think stocks and bonds) in various risk classifications. His theory was that riskier investments, like certain classes of stocks or high-risk bonds, create greater opportunities for profit (see Chapter 16). Conversely, volatility drag lowers one's profits in riskier investments[4]. As you saw in previous chapters, risk or volatility drag is a serious matter.

Markowitz was able to prove that holding a mix of investments types in different risk classes enables you to significantly lower your overall risk and maximize your upward profitability. He proved that if some of your investments drop, your overall nest egg could still rise as the total was bolstered by the other investments you owned that did well. This phenomena dampens the impact of volatility drag on your portfolio's value. Even if all your investments dropped, most would do so at various (slower) rates, which still dampens volatility drag. This theory assumes most people want their investments to be as profitable as possible, while still being as safe as possible.

Eugene Fama conceived the Efficient Market Hypothesis (EMH) in 1970, winning the Nobel Prize in 2013 for his theory. Drawing upon the work of Francis Galton, Fama's theory states that all the known information about a stock is correctly reflected in the company's current stock price, which means that all the investors who own this stock have already considered all the information that the general public can know and this information is correctly reflected by the current price of the stock[5]. As a company's market position changes in its industry, or the broader economic conditions evolve, it creates price fluctuations based on everyone's evaluation of this new information. Therefore, a profit cannot be obtained by evaluating new information to look for either an undervalued stock purchase or the sale of an overvalued stock—above the overall market's gain or loss.

John C. Bogle created the first index fund in 1975 for Vanguard Investments[6]. The point of index funds is that they provide an easy way to purchase a great deal of diversity and some protection against diversifiable risk. It also takes the human factor of emotion out of the equation. This investment is considered a passive investment because there are no active decisions being made by a fund manager to buy or sell stocks. The fund manager merely mirrors the index and fees are significantly less. When fees are considered, and they always should be, it is reported that index funds perform better than 91 percent of all actively managed funds. An actively managed fund is where a manager regularly buys and sells investments inside the fund in an attempt to create a greater profit higher than the general market's movement. Typically, active funds charge higher fees for the all the active management to (hopefully) benefit the fund.

Every day someone is predicting a market downturn (a trend toward lower stock prices in the stock market called a bear market). Sometimes, these investors are famous people and other times, the predictions are made by prestigious large investment firms or famous fund managers. These folks use detailed analyses to come to a conclusion that the market will soon suffer a downturn that is right around the corner. Sometimes these financial professionals (or others) profit if you believe them and begin selling your stocks, while other times, they just wanted to get publicity. The point is that people predict downturns or upturns in the stock market every day. History has proven most of their predictions wrong.

Other times, people have predicted terrible outcomes depending on a presidential election. During President Obama's presidency, numerous pundits predicted dire downturns and a possible stock market crash. I still made a lot of money by maintaining my portfolio mix. People are now predicting terrible economic outcomes with President Trump. I am still making money on a rising stock market (called a bull market) and by maintaining my portfolio mix of investments. Don't get wrapped up in politics, at least as far as your investments are concerned. All presidents and politicians know that their success is partially dependent upon how our economy is performing and are motivated to keep it functioning well, which is true even if they won't admit that it is important. Terrible economic conditions also have an impact on politicians and their families as well.

As mad as it makes the hobby stock pickers, TV predictors, financial pundits, political analysts or Wall Street money managers, the real truth is no one knows the market's direction in the short term. I feel comfortable suggesting the long-term direction of stocks is up, just considering inflation if nothing else. Of course, our entire economy could collapse or a meteor could destroy the earth. Both outcomes are possible, but remain highly unlikely. As my dad used to tell me when I made a dire prediction about my future or the economy, "Yeah, but what if it doesn't happen?" What he meant is that you shouldn't worry about things that are beyond your control.

To know the short-term direction of markets (less than three years), would take a detailed knowledge of almost countless subjects and the future actions of others, including but not limited to:

- Future Federal Reserve actions
- The science of economics as it relates to our current economic conditions

- Imminent geopolitical events
- The direction and health of our world economy
- A detailed understanding of investor psychology
- Weather conditions as they impact our economy and the world economy
- Future business cycles' impact on corporate profitability
- Future Wall Street misconduct scandals
- Technology changes
- Changes in our government's policies
- Future news and events not listed here

Some people make stock market predictions for nefarious purposes, while others make predictions with the best of intentions. Predictions might likely be accurate if it were not for the fact that everything in our world is in constant flux, making future predictions about the short-term market highly improbable.

Many people feel that studying the past helps us to predict the future. As it relates to stock prices or the economy as a whole, that view is an illusion. Thankfully, our investments are not prisoners of the past and it would be awful if our investments were forever governed by past events! The future can be different and the past does not accurately allow you to predict all future stock price directions. It makes much more sense to worry about the things we can control in investing such as:

- Creating a portfolio with a mix of investments (stocks and bonds) at your comfort level
- Keep all investment fees as low as possible.
- Utilize a variety of index funds as your primary investment vehicles to obtain diversity and the lowest possible fees.
- Minimize taxes which are simply another fee structure.

I know the stock-picking crowd is having a fit with this chapter. They believe they can accurately pick undervalued stocks or predict stock market downturns and upturns. They point to Robert Shiller who won the Nobel Prize for his work in 2013 with stocks' price-earnings ratio (P/E) and price fluctuations. Like the title suggests, you divide the price of the stock by the corporation's earnings per share. Price per share $40/$5 amount of earnings = P/E of 8. You would then subtract any dividends you received that year. Shiller believed some stocks were overvalued and had high P/Es. Undervalued stocks had low P/Es. The problem is, some company stocks are considered a great deal with a P/E of 8, while other company stocks have a P/E of 30 and are still considered great stock deals. Also, Shiller's predictions of the stock market direction based on high or low P/Es were wrong as recently as May of 2018[7]. As an example, he predicted a broad market downturn last year, yet the stock market has significantly gone up. Will he be right in the future? Who knows? You could flip a coin and even that predictive method will eventually be right.

Worrying about the things you can't control, like stock market direction, is a pointless endeavor. Don't waste your time and effort, because you have more important things to do with your life. Concentrate on what you can control. Focus on your goals. Keep the debt monster at bay by following your budget. Continue to save your money to feed your investments. Keep your portfolio within the mix and percentages you have chosen. Taking these stair steps will keep you on the surest path to financial success.

EUGENE FAMA
WON THE NOBEL PRIZE IN 2013
FOR HIS EFFICIENT MARKET THEORY

"THE FUTURE DIRECTION OF STOCKS, OR THE STOCK MARKET DIRECTION AS A WHOLE, CANNOT BE PREDICTED IN THE SHORT TERM (2 YEARS OR LESS)"

50% CHANCE STOCKS GO UP

50% CHANCE STOCKS GO DOWN

NEVER BELIEVE STOCK MARKET PREDICTIONS!

TO KNOW MARKET DIRECTION, YOU WOULD HAVE TO KNOW:

1. FEDERAL RESERVE ACTIONS IN THE FUTURE
2. ECONOMIC EVENTS IN THE FUTURE
3. GEOPOLITICAL EVENTS IN THE FUTURE
4. DIRECTION OF WORLD ECONOMY
5. INVESTOR PSYCHOLOGY
6. FUTURE WEATHER EVENTS
7. NORMAL BUSINESS CYCLE IMPACT
8. CORRUPTION SCANDALS IN THE FUTURE
9. TECHNOLOGY CHANGES
10. CHANGES IN GOVERNMENT POLICY

NO ONE CAN POSSIBLY KNOW ALL THIS STUFF!

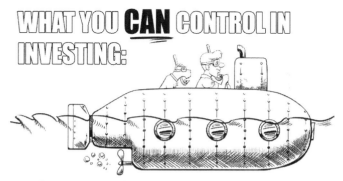

WHAT YOU **CAN** CONTROL IN INVESTING:

1. CONTROL YOUR MIX OF STOCKS & BONDS

2. KEEP FEES LOW

3. USE OF INDEX MUTUAL FUNDS FOR SAFETY & LOW FEES

4. MINIMIZE TAXES

18

Investing: Efficient Market Theory Supports Index Funds

"Efficiency is anything that scores."
—Bruce Lee

Using index funds and creating a portfolio of diverse investments with the persistent investing of your savings over time can turn your nest egg into a multi-million dollar portfolio! Numerous methods and theories exist to help you grow your nest egg, but I prefer the methods designed and used by Nobel Prize-winning economists over the last century. As I mentioned earlier, the Efficient Market Hypothesis, conceived by Eugene Fama, earned him the Nobel Prize in 2013 for his groundbreaking theory that all the publicly known information about a stock (representing company ownership) is correctly reflected in the company's current stock price[1]. All the investors who own this stock have already considered all the information that the general public can know and that information is correctly reflected by the price of the stock, or the price the stock is currently being bought and sold at any moment in time.

The Efficient Market Hypothesis bolsters the idea of purchasing index mutual funds, which are passive investments (no decisions are being made by an investment manager) that track large indexes of stocks and greatly lower your fees. Indexes are simply made-up groupings of stocks designed by stock analysts or the financial press to track the performance of our economy—either as a whole or in certain sectors[2]. For example, Standard and Poor's 500 (S&P 500) tracks most large corporations in our American economy. The Dow Jones Industrial Average (DJIA) is composed of 30 large corporations commonly traded on the New York Stock Exchange. It was created by Charles Dow, and Edward Jones[3] and is now the most commonly discussed stock market index in the world.

When you purchase shares in an index mutual fund, you are purchasing a mutual fund that mirrors a particular index in the financial market. Here are some well-known indexes that are famous for tracking our economy or sectors of our economy:

- Dow Jones Industrial Average: 30 influential companies on New York Stock Exchange
- Standard and Poor's 500: top 500 largest companies in the U.S.
- Nasdaq Composite (Nasdaq): technology stocks
- Vanguard Midcap Index Fund: mid-sized companies across market sectors
- Russell 2000: a small cap index (small companies)
- S&P 600: small cap index
- Wilshire 500: tracks 6,700 companies (a composite of all U.S. companies)

If one company goes out of business or changes in size, another company replaces it. An index mutual fund mirrors the chosen index in its stock ownership and changes as the index changes. There are many different indexes and some of them perform better in different stages of our economy—referring to times of expansion or retraction in our economy.

The only way to beat the market's averages (as reflected by indexes) is to take higher risks[4]. You recall that higher risk produces greater opportunity for a higher profit but also produces wider swings in profitability—volatility drag. Most of the time, market professionals and individual stock pickers underperform the market index due to a variety of factors:

- Drag caused by the volatility of higher risk investments to make larger profits than the averages reflected by index mutual funds
- Fees created and passed on to you from the buying and selling of individual stocks inside the fund
- Index funds have been shown to outperform 90 percent of actively managed mutual funds in any single year[5].
- Beats all actively managed fund for similar investments when compared over long time periods[6]
- The fund faithfully follows the index and their strategy does not deviate as they frequently do in actively managed funds.
- Instant diversification with the purchase of an index mutual fund
- Using index mutual funds significantly simplify your investment strategy to the point that virtually anyone can be successful over the long haul.

The last point in the list above is particularly important. Most people, with the exception of personal finance nerds, don't want to spend hours a day analyzing various stocks and looking for good investments. They want to "set it and forget it" for a while. Additionally, I have never believed that it is possible to compete with Wall Street high-profile investment companies. This group can frequently move the financial markets by buying and selling large quantities of assets. Our market is so large, however, their moves only temporarily impact stock or bond prices.

Large Wall Street investment firms have computer programs that monitor the market at all times, looking for certain patterns. When these patterns appear, they can instantly buy or sell stocks via their computer connections to make a quick profit. Computer trades have priority, occurring much faster than you could ever personally respond via a requested buy or sell order for individual stocks[7].

Certain investors on Wall Street have many connections that you and I will never have. They hear things, know things and are more informed than the average investor could ever hope to be. Typically, this is the group that goes from government to Wall Street and back to government. You can't compete with that kind of handicap and neither can your friendly neighborhood investment advisor[8].

Want to make more money than 90 percent of the people investing in our stock market? Use index funds as your primary investment vehicles. Some people will disagree with the methods I favor (the individual stock-picking crowd), but did those people who disagree with me create their own million-plus portfolio of investments while earning middle-class wages and raising a family of five? If they did something similar, then I am happy to hear what they have to say. Keep an open mind and consider the information I am providing. Index funds, purchased in a mutual fund format, is an easy, safer way to invest your hard-earned savings!

WHY BUY INDEX FUNDS?

1. PASSIVE INVESTMENT THAT JUST FOLLOWS INDEX

2. LOW FEES SINCE NO STOCK RESEARCH OR STOCK PICKING REQUIRED

3. THE ONLY WAY TO BEAT MARKET AVERAGES (INDEXES) IS TO TAKE MORE RISK. MORE RISK CREATES VOLATILITY DRAG & INCREASES FEES FOR RESEARCH AND BUYING AND SELLING!

MOST FAMOUS INDEXES:

-DOW JONES INDUSTRIAL AVERAGE (DJIA)

-STANDARD & POORS 500 (S&P 500- LARGE COMPANIES)

-NASDAQ COMPOSITE (NASDAQ- TECH STOCKS)

-VANGUARD MIDCAP FUND (MIDCAP STOCKS)

-RUSSELL 2000 (GROUP OF SMALL COMPANIES)

-S & P 600 SMALL CAP (SMALL COMPANIES)

-WILLSHIRE 500 (6700 COMPANIES OF VARIOUS SIZES)

19

Investing: Build a Diverse Portfolio to Increase Profit and Decrease Risk

"An investment in knowledge always pays the best interest."
—Benjamin Franklin

Want to keep your investments as safe as possible while at the same time maximizing your investing profits? Then you certainly want to learn how to construct your own investment portfolio[1]. Harry Markowitz won the Nobel Prize in 1990 for his Modern Portfolio Theory, which was so powerful that it virtually reshaped modern investing. Markowitz discovered, among other things, that your individual investment is not as important as how your investments interact with your entire portfolio. An investor should own a wide mix of financial assets to create a diverse portfolio with the goal of creating additional safety and increasing profit.

The idea of a diverse portfolio is that you own many different types or classifications of investments. If one investment starts going down in value, your overall portfolio value will likely still increase because the other investments will make up for the loss with their profits. Using this method, your portfolio's total value (not necessarily its individual investments) is more likely to continue to grow. Asset types take turns giving investors the highest returns, depending on economic conditions. This method acts like a parachute on a package dropped from a plane, slowing the downward fall of the package (your portfolio).

The goal is to pick a mix of investments that do not move in correlation (or in tandem) with each other. In this context, correlation is a statistical measure. It signifies the degree to which two investments move in relation to each other. Investments are assigned a value between 1 and -1, called the correlation coefficient. The 1 value simply implies that two investment prices move in tandem with each other. The -1 value implies the two investment prices move in opposite directions. So there is either a negative or a positive correlation between your various investments.

Investment advisors use a complex math formula to set up their portfolios. You are not likely to find this level of detail necessary. You should know that you need a group of bond-type investments or interest-bearing instruments and a group of equities (stocks) that will move in the opposite direction of your bonds as the economy goes through various stages in its constantly evolving business cycle.

You also need to know that the mix of bonds and stocks creates your level of risk. Stocks are riskier than bonds (See Chapter 16). Stock prices vary over time—sometimes wildly—and there is no guarantee a stock will be worth more than you paid for it. Choose the mix of bonds (less risky) and stocks (more risky) that you are comfortable with. It could be a 50/50 mix, which is what we have and is called the couch potato portfolio, or you might be bolder and want 60 percent stocks and 40 percent bonds. The younger you are, the more aggressive you can be with a higher mix of stocks. Remember, the money you invest first grows the most over time. If you are young, be relentlessly aggressive by owning far more stocks. If your time horizon is 20 to 30 years until you need or want the money, you actually have little to fear.

After you decide on the mix of stocks and bonds you are comfortable with, then you should decide upon the subclasses of stocks that makes you feel comfortable, such as small cap (cap stands for capitalization which is the value of all that company's stocks taken as a whole), large cap, international, etc. The same choices are needed with bonds. Pick a variety of different bond classes within your mix. My wife and I prefer index mutual funds. Using a mix of investments has been shown to increase overall profits by reducing volatility drag. As you recall from the chapter on risk, investments with higher risk (like stocks) create greater opportunity for larger profits. However, higher-risk investments come with volatile, erratic price movements. A mix of stocks and bonds reduces risk drag in most cases.

The mix of stocks and bonds also reduces both nonsystematic risk (risk of owning a single company or a single industry) and systematic risk (risk of our economy having a downturn in the current business cycle). Of course, the inverse correlation between stocks and bonds does not always function perfectly. Once in a while, sadly, both bonds and stocks move downward in price. So the old axiom in investing remains true—no investment is ever a sure thing!

Think of an investment portfolio as pot pie. We are going to bake a flavorful pot pie by using an old family recipe. You need to put great ingredients into your pie like beef and various vegetables so it will be delicious. A pot pie is a terrific analogy for an investment portfolio. Instead of tasty ingredients, we are going to use a variety of investments that do not all move in correlation with each other. You should pick a mix of stocks and bonds (and some other assets) to create your portfolio. My wife and I have approximately 50 percent in bonds or in stable value return investments and 50 percent in stock funds. If you are younger, you should probably pick a more aggressive mix with a larger percentage of stocks.

Over time, as some investments go down or do not rise as fast as others. The overall mix of the portfolio begins to stray from your initial percentage mix. When this happens, you rebalance your portfolio, which means you bring your investments back to your chosen percentage mix by selling some of the financial assets that are doing well (above your preset percentage limits) and buying the ones that are not doing as well (the price has gone down in value and now below your preset percentage limits). This actually forces you to buy low and then sell high, which increases your profitability over the long run. This is not an attempt to "time" the market, it is just assuring your portfolio mix remains consistent with your comfort level. We start to consider rebalancing when the portfolio travels four percent or higher away from our chosen mix while other people are just fine with rebalancing annually.

Failure to buy a variety of asset types and maintain the mix you have chosen can lead to tragic results. Initially, we didn't bother with this step. Instead, we simply bought the mutual funds that had the best returns in our employers' 401(k)s. It was all great until the market hit a significant downturn in the late 1990s. It was at that time I learned that the top funds all invested in almost the exact same things. Since we didn't have a variety of asset types, most of our investments were impacted with few investment classes to slow this drop. This cost us around $100,000 and we learned a hard lesson about diversifying our investments. When the next downturn hit, our diversity limited our losses just as it was designed. Also, rebalancing created large and significant profits when the market recovered a couple of years later.

Just like we put a variety of ingredients in our pot pie, we need a variety of different classes of investments within various investment categories. In the business cycle (discussed in the next chapter), we learn that the economy goes through various phases. During each phase, different investments tend do better than others. Look at the indexed stock fund examples listed below. In these examples, the term market capitalization translates to the total value of all outstanding shares of a company. Larger companies have large market capitalization. Index funds are created to follow indexes of stocks or bonds in various size categories such as:

- Large caps are companies with 10 billion dollars or above in market capitalization (number of company's out-standing shares multiplied by the stock price), typically do well during a recession and are considered lower risk.
- Mid-caps are companies between two and 10 billion dol-lars in market capitalization and typically shine during periods of inflation with rising prices.
- Small caps have less than two billion dollars in market capitalization, are typically the first to recover from a shrinking economy and have the ability to achieve large gains at any time.

Sometimes investors like to mix up their categories related to where the funds are located, such as:

- Domestic stock fund
- Foreign fund
- Emerging market stock fund

For the other part of your portfolio, you will need bond funds or interest-bearing investments such as:

- U.S. Treasury Bonds
- U.S. Treasury Inflation Protection Bonds (TIPS are a special type of bond where you receive interest and possibly additional money that is tied to a rising inflation rate).
- REIT (Real Estate Investment Trust), a fund that buys shares of commercial companies that own income-producing real estate such as apartment buildings, hospitals, medical buildings, retail buildings, etc.

We own a small amount of a commodities investment fund, which deal with raw materials like gold, other industrial metals, currencies and crops—tangible items that can be touched. In stages of our economy when inflation starts to rear its ugly head, commodities are a great hedge (hedge in investing implies that it offsets losses if they occur and protects your portfolio from loss) as other investments struggle to keep up with inflation. Commodities are negatively correlated with both stocks and bonds.

This is our current portfolio mix, which has worked very well for us and we plan to keep it well into the future:

23% Large caps
12% Small caps
11% International companies
23% Treasury bonds
23% Stable value fund
5% REIT
3% Commodities
= 100% Portfolio

The younger you are, the more risk you can take (increase the stock portion of your portfolio). The early money that you invest has the opportunity to grow the most over time. As you get older, your pot of money has grown, so you can begin to scale back the number of stocks you have in favor of the safer, interest-bearing investments like bonds because you have limited time for the market to recover from major declines.

Remember the income streams we talked about at the beginning of this book? The more diverse your income streams, the more aggressive (more stocks) you can afford to have in your asset allocation. Income streams, like a pension or military disability, are considered fixed income investments—much like some long-term bonds. Even though I am in my early 60s, we maintain a 50/50 mix of investments because of our various income streams. If it were not for these income streams, we might be less aggressive at our age. Frequently, people in their 50s and 60s are too conservative. Unless you are in your late 80s or 90s, you are still going to need your investments to grow as you age. You could live a very long time and you don't want to run out of money. Your portfolio can even continue to grow even after you start using it. The key is to typically only remove four percent or less annually.

Look at a few of the many asset allocation examples online to get a feel for devising your portfolio. You can build a hypothetical portfolio online at Meta Chart[2]. Also, this is an area where your brokerage house can assist you. Many advisors are troublesome because they only want to sell you high-fee investments. After years of searching, we finally found an advisor at Fidelity to bounce ideas off of and who makes us feel comfortable. She doesn't try to sell us anything! She simply helps us with our asset allocation via her excellent computer models and suggests additional low-fee options to add to our portfolio (these type of financial advisors are out there, you just have to look around to find them). Mostly, she just encourages us to stay on track. An advisor like that is worth his or her weight in gold!

Brokerage houses have asset allocation models online, which are generally pretty useful. Just remember to choose the lower-cost option of index funds when you can. The construction of your portfolio is where you put most of your efforts, not individual stock picking. That principle is very important. Spend your time working on your portfolio and not so much on individual stocks or bonds.

Someone usually brings up the subject of target date funds about this time. A target date fund, according to the stated objectives, does all the portfolio work for you. The fund automatically starts out heavily invested in stocks and higher risk investments. Over time, the investments become more and more conservative (safer) with bond-type investments as you age. At first glance, this seems like a great deal and a much easier way to create a diverse portfolio. You simply buy a target date fund and someone else has to worry about the investment mix. My experience and the experience of many others have led to the observation that the fees for target date funds are higher and the performance is typically below what you can accomplish on your own[3]. You can usually do better than this using the strategies we previously discussed.

You should not give much worry or thought to what the market is doing today, tomorrow or even a couple of years down the road. Think about the long-term instead. If you get worried about your investments, make sure your portfolio mix is at your pre-chosen ratio. If the world is ready to end, keep your investments at your pre-chosen mix. If the market is going great guns, keep your portfolio at its pre-chosen mix. If you receive reports that a meteor is likely to strike the earth and destroy everything, then keep your portfolio at its pre-chosen mix. Please don't bother listening to the financial press discussing market direction. They know less about it than you now do.

HARRY MARKOWITZ WON THE NOBEL PRIZE IN 1990 FOR MODERN PORTFOLIO THEORY!

LIKE A POT PIE WITH A MIX OF MANY DIFFERENT INGREDIENTS, A PORTFOLIO IS A MIX OF MANY DIFFERENT INVESTMENTS!

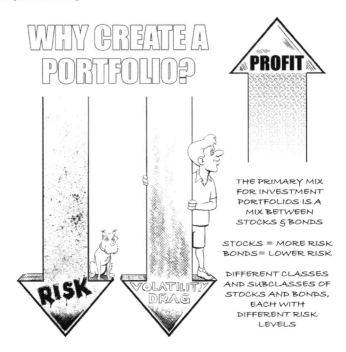

WHY CREATE A PORTFOLIO?

RISK

VOLATILITY DRAG

PROFIT

THE PRIMARY MIX FOR INVESTMENT PORTFOLIOS IS A MIX BETWEEN STOCKS & BONDS

STOCKS = MORE RISK
BONDS = LOWER RISK

DIFFERENT CLASSES AND SUBCLASSES OF STOCKS AND BONDS, EACH WITH DIFFERENT RISK LEVELS

PORTFOLIO

-INCREASES SAFETY THROUGH DIVERSIFICATION

-INCREASES PROFIT BY REDUCING VOLATILITY DRAG

23% Treasury Bonds

23% Large Co.

23% Stable Return Investment

12% Small Co.

11% International

3% Commodities

5% REIT

REAL ESTATE INVESTMENT TRUST

20

Investing: Business Cycles

"Buy when everyone else is selling and hold until everyone else is buying. That's not just a catchy slogan. It's the very essence of successful investing."

—J. Paul Getty

D o you want to buy your clothes when they are being sold for a premium, or would you like to buy your clothes when they are on sale? Even people who are not really bargain hunters strive to not pay full price for clothing. After all, clothes are an expensive part of your budget! In fact, when buying clothing, most people check out the sales racks to see if they can find what they want at a discounted price, which is a great cost-saving strategy. One of the nicest things about buying clothes on sale is that it is the exact same stuff you would have paid premium prices for if you had gone to the store at a different time[1.]

When it comes to buying investments, however, bargain seeking seems to get all jumbled up in investors' brains. When stocks are hot (doing very well and going up in price), people try to buy them! Essentially, by the time you hear that an investment is really hot and want to buy it, you end up paying a premium with hardly any gain in the short term. You can't wait to buy investments when that particular investment class has already become a hot commodity, which is why you should own many different categories of investments. That way, you already own whatever class of investment suddenly becomes hot for the next few weeks, months or years!

Conversely, when investments fall into the basement due to the latest news stories and the media begins to speculate that it is the end of the world, investors get frightened and sell their investment(s). In other words, people tend to buy when the market is expensive and sell after it goes into the basement. This is the exact opposite of our goal! Wouldn't we all like to make money rather than give it away to other investors?

Financial markets, like stocks, go up and down all the time, which is nothing to get concerned about. If the stock market goes down more than six percent or so, I start wondering if I can get the disfavored investments on sale and start checking my current asset allocation mix. I never panic about falling stocks. I also never suggest jumping all in to stocks. I will usually check to see if rebalancing my portfolio is in order. If so, I sell investment funds whose total percentages are too high and buy those investments that have dropped below my target percentages. In other words, I bring my investment portfolio back to the parameters I previously set.

Did you know that most stock gains typically occur only once or twice a year? It is never a steady gain over time. Most of the time, stock gains are small or dull. A couple of times a year, or even once a year, the stock market makes dramatic leaps forward. You can't wait until that happens to try to buy stocks!

These are the reasons we own different investments and different sub-classes of those investments. As I stated in the last chapter, different investments do well during different periods of the business cycle. A business cycle is the expansion and contraction of our economy and is tracked through the GDP (Gross Domestic Product), which is America's production of all goods and services. Two down quarters of a GDP is an official recession. GDP is tracked by the U.S. Bureau of Labor Statistics[2] (BLS.gov). A recession is also gauged by the unemployment rate. During a recession, unemployment rises while the GDP falls. Here are the official stages of the business cycle:

- Expansion
- Peak
- Recession
- Trough
- Recovery

As the economy goes through the expansion phase, stock prices begin to increase. When a recession slide begins, stocks sell-off and their prices start to go down. At the low point or trough portion of the cycle, stocks linger in a malaise and the prices hover at low levels. It all starts over again with the next economic expansion.

Bonds act differently during the business cycle. As an expansion begins, investors begin to sell off their bonds to buy stocks. Bond prices drop. During the recession phase, investors sell stocks and flee to the safety of bonds. Bond prices begin to rise. As you may have deduced by now, stocks move in the opposite direction of bonds—at least in theory. Sometimes, painfully, both investments seem to move in tandem for a short time.

Since the 1940s, there have been 11 to 14 downturns in our economy, depending on who is doing the counting[3]. Some of these downturns were the result of investment bubbles bursting— like the housing market or tech stock crash. Other times, a recession was caused by the general slowing of our economy or excessive borrowing. Business cycles are normal and are not going away. An expanding economy, thankfully, is our default setting, although some expansions may be slow and lethargic. Recessions, thankfully, typically last only last from 11 to 22 months. When the financial press reports that the current recession is the end of our financial world, they are showing their ignorance.

Take advantage of business cycles by using dollar-cost averaging to build wealth over time. Dollar-cost averaging is a simple technique that entails investing your savings, at regular intervals, over a long period of time. If you have a 401(k) retirement plan, you're already using this strategy when you invest your weekly or bi-weekly paycheck into your various investment accounts. When stocks are down, your money goes further and buys more stocks. When the stock market is up, your money doesn't goes as far and buys fewer stocks.

To summarize, you can expect several downturns during your investing lifetime. If you have a mixed portfolio of investments, never fear downturns. Downturns for a long-term investor are great opportunities. A down market creates a golden opportunity to make money by buying investments that are essentially on sale. Just remember to rebalance your portfolio back to your chosen mix ratio at least annually. Take a long view of investing and never get too excited by a down year or two. If listening to the financial media upsets you or makes you anxious, then don't listen to them. Selling all your stocks when the stock market falls is a grievous error and it only enriches other investors. Never concentrate on what the market is doing today or even this year. Instead, concentrate on keeping your portfolio at your chosen mix of investments, continue to invest over time and don't panic!

BUSINESS CYCLES = EXPANSION & CONTRACTION OF OUR ECONOMY
BUSINESS CYCLES ARE NORMAL. 11 TO 14 SINCE THE 1940'S DEPENDING ON WHO COUNTS!

EXPANSION = STOCK PRICE INCREASE
RECESSION = STOCK PRICE GO DOWN
TROUGH = STOCK PRICES HOVER AT A REDUCED PRICE

BOND PRICES ARE SLIGHTLY DIFFERENT

EXPANSION: STOCK PRICES RISE. INVESTORS MOVE TO STOCKS. BONDS ARE SOLD TO BUY STOCKS. BOND PRICES START TO DROP!

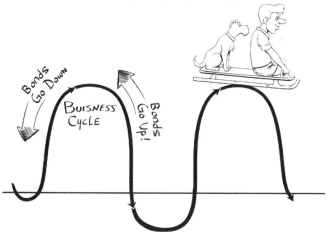

RECESSION: INVESTORS FLEE FROM STOCKS & BUY BONDS. BOND PRICES RISE!

IF STOCK PRICES FALL, PANIC SETS IN & EVERYONE SELLS!

IF STOCK PRICES ARE HIGH, EVERYONE BUYS AT TOP DOLLAR!

=LOSE MONEY

DON'T FOLLOW THE HERD!

THE GOAL IS TO MAKE MONEY, NOT GIVE IT AWAY!

WHEN STOCK PRICES ARE LOW, THEY ARE ON SALE!
SAME STOCKS AS BEFORE, ONLY AT LOWER PRICE!
CONSIDER BUYING...

WHEN STOCKS GO HIGH, HIGH & HIGHER THEY ARE HOT ITEMS
& ARE SELLING AT A PREMIUM! CONSIDER SELLING...

ACTUALLY, JUST REBALANCE YOUR PORTFOLIO
BACK TO THE RATIO YOU CHOSE & THAT WILL
ACCOMPLISH THE SAME THING!

REBALANCE AT LEAST ANNUALLY!

21

Summary

Do You Have the Grit to Achieve Your Dreams?

"Believe that you can and decide that you will!"
—Larry Faulkner

This book is about increasing your wealth, expanding your free-dom and substantially increasing your chances of achieving your most treasured dreams. This is not a book about retirement. Long before you achieve the goal of financial independence, you will have put yourself squarely in the driver's seat of your life by cre-ating abundant monetary resources. With those kind of resources, you will be better off than the vast majority of our population, comprised primarily of low financial achievers.

Living a different, more productive lifestyle will require grit and perseverance—especially at first. Most people, of course, never develop the necessary work ethic or learned the value of perseverance in the face of serious obstacles. Most people blunder through their financial lives and obtain unsatisfactory outcomes and scarce financial resources—forever. What separates you from these people are the goals you have set and your commitment to achieving progress each and every day toward those goals. Of course, to attain those goals, you must take responsibility for your financial outcomes via the ironclad rule of responsibility. You absolutely must believe that you can do this. I did it! Others have done it! You can get control of your life and achieve the freedom you have longed for! You must simply decide to make financial abundance happen and then go do it.

Your job is important and requires hard work. Make it count by maximizing your ability to earn and save the income you produce. Get the most from your job financially and then figure out how to create additional income streams. Diverse income streams are the seeds of your future prosperity. You now know that your career, no matter what it might be, has an expiration date and the income you earn during your working career is limited. Maximize your income early and make every dime count!

No one likes budgeting, but budgeting is the difference between high financial performance and a mediocre outcome. If you fail to budget now, you will absolutely budget later when the debt monster forces you to live with very meager financial means. Either way, you will end up budgeting. So budget early, make your early sacrifices count and accelerate your life forward. If you fail to take action, you will simply keep repeating the same money management mistakes over and over again in an endless loop!

The next step on to financial independence is reducing debt, which is a subcategory of budgeting. Debt is a monster and robs your future, while keeping you poor in the present. School debt is especially insidious and robs you of the ability to save serious money early in your working career, when saving counts the most.

The money you save early in your career is the money that grows the most over your lifetime. You absolutely must reduce your debt by creating and working through your own debt reduction plan.

Take the next stair step on your way to your financial independence by saving. The very point of creating additional income and then budgeting is to create even more savings. The more you save now, the more options you will have in your future. In a sense, you are deferring gratification today in exchange for a much better tomorrow.

You understand that you can never save your way to wealth. To create significant financial independence requires you to take the next stair step—invest your hard-earned savings. Investing is not complicated or difficult and certainly not boring. It is actually a lot of fun, as you will soon see, and much easier than everything you had to do to get to the point where you can now invest your savings. After utilizing your blood, sweat, tears and wit to create income, investing is relatively simple and fun!

The alternative, of course, is that you spend all your days doing things you don't particularly want to do. You become imprisoned by your growing financial debt monster. All of your ideas for your life are put on hold—likely forever. Eventually, you accept the fact that you will live a life of financial servitude with very limited financial resources for as long as you live! I want more for you. You must want more for yourself! Leave your self-made debt prison and run toward prosperity.

It is quite the dichotomy that the process of building wealth actually starts deep in our brains. It all begins with believing that you can create wealth to improve your life. From that belief, you then develop the necessary knowledge base to guide your actions in the physical world. Building prosperity is also greatly dependent upon your attitude. Without maintaining a positive attitude, you won't have the patience and ability to overcome the roadblocks and setbacks we all experience. It is also a dichotomy that the more we mess with our investments, the less successful they typically become. Buying and selling individual investments creates unnecessary fees. Instead, you now know to concentrate on setting and maintaining your portfolio mix of investments. Even doing this chore annually is usually just fine.

Essentially, we are going to win in the financial markets by not playing, or by playing only by our own rules. We are going to win by keeping our investing fees low. We are going to win by avoiding tax liability as much as possible. We are going to win by continuing to invest monthly and utilizing cost averaging over time. We are going to win by cutting out financial advisors and keeping their portion (taken in fees) in our investments earning us even more money. We are going to win by having a mixed portfolio of various investment types, categories and levels of risk. No matter what is hot at the moment, we will already own it. We are going to win by rebalancing our portfolio annually, or when it travels five percent or six percent away from our chosen investment mix. This technique will force us to buy low and sell high!

Remember, the early pain of traversing those stair steps composed of goal-setting, creating income, budgeting, saving and then investing to achieve financial independence is temporary. Eventually, the entire process becomes so much easier with practice, patience and perseverance in the face of obstacles. The only way you will ever get what you want in life is to set goals and then do what is necessary to achieve them—within legal and moral boundaries, of course. I believe you can create unparalleled freedom in your life. Now the question is, do you have the grit and determination necessary to get this job done?

BELIEVE THAT YOU CAN AND DECIDE THAT YOU WILL!

WHAT YOU NEED
TO SUCCEED:

-GRIT
-DETERMINATION
-WORK ETHIC
-PERSERVERANCE
-POSITIVE ATTITUDE
-PATIENCE
-KNOWLEDGE
-CONFIDENCE
"BELIEVE YOU CAN"

INVEST

SAVING

BUDGET

INCOME
CREATION

SET
GOALS

STAIRSTEPS TO
FINANCIAL
INDEPENDENCE

Citations

Chapter 1: The Point Of It All

[1] https://www.businessnewsdaily.com/2871-how-most-millionaires-got-rich.html

[2] http://money.com/money/5023038/millionaire-population-united-states-world/

Chapter 3: Goal-Setting

[1] https://www.amazon.com/Messages-Your-Future-Financial-Professional-ebook/dp/B01E4NVUNY

[2] https://www.psychologytoday.com/us/blog/pieces-mind/201605/overcoming-obstacles

[3] https://link.springer.com/article/10.1007/s10902-016-9750-0

Chapter 4: Create Income

[1] https://pdfs.semanticscholar.org/61e7/0a6cde51efa1e04ac5ea018781cd51bada35.pdf

[2] https://nypost.com/2019/05/28/world-health-organization-now-considers-burnout-a-condition/

[3] https://www.statnews.com/2017/03/14/depression-burnout-doctors-debt/

Chapter 5: Create Income: Ramping Up Your Income

[1] https://smallbiztrends.com/2019/03/startup-statistics-small-business.html

[2] Ibid.

Chapter 6: Budgeting: Live A Different Lifestyle

[1] https://money.cnn.com/2016/10/24/pf/financial-mistake-budget/index.html

[2] https://www.cnbc.com/2019/05/10/62-percent-of-millennials-say-they-are-living-paycheck-to-paycheck.html

[3] https://www.cnbc.com/2019/01/09/shutdown-highlights-that-4-in-5-us-workers-live-paycheck-to-paycheck.html

[4] Warren, Elizabeth, Amelia Warren-Tyagi. *All Your Worth: The Ultimate Lifetime Money Plan.* New York: Free Press A Division Of Simon and Shuster, Inc., 2005. Ebook Edition. Chp. 1.

[5] Faulkner, Larry. *Messages From Your Future: The Seven Rules for Financial, Personal and Professional Success.* Dayton: Faulkner Integrated Tactics, 2016. 13-30

Chapter 7: The Why And The How Of The Tasks Ahead

[1] https://www.census.gov/library/stories/2018/09/highest-median-household-income-on-record.html

[2] https://www.aarp.org/work/working-at-50-plus/info-2018/forced-retirement.html

[3] https://cutt.ly/swWaD2

Chapter 8: Finances And Your Significant Other

[1] https://www.independent.co.uk/news/business/news/money-marriage-end-divorce-day-relationships-personal-finances-slater-gordon-a8147921.html

[2] https://www.psychologytoday.com/us/articles/200403/marriage-math

[3] https://pdfs.semanticscholar.org/657c/7b20e4c3fbd033bb5a-8093073f898aa971e0.pdf

Chapter 9: Do You Want To Be A Financial Winner Or A Loser?

[1] https://www.magnifymoney.com/blog/news/average-american-savings/

[2] https://www.schwab.com/resource-center/insights/content/does-financial-planning-help

[3] https://www.marketwatch.com/story/most-young-americans-are-living-on-the-edge-financially-2018-08-27

[4] https://www.usfinancialcapability.org/downloads/FINRA_GFLEC_Investor_Knowledge_Report.pdf?utm_source=MM&utm_medium=email&utm_campaign=S%5FIPC%5F-News%5F103119%5FFINAL

[5] https://www.investopedia.com

[6] https://www.investopedia.com/investing/can-you-make-money-stocks/

Chapter 10: Debt Monsters

[1] https://undebt.it

[2] Ibid

[3] mint.com

[4] https://www.youneedabudget.com

Chapter 11: Saving

[1] https://www.bea.gov/data/income-saving/personal-saving-rate

[2] https://www.statista.com/statistics/246234/personal-savings-rate-in-the-united-states/

[3] https://www.visualcapitalist.com

[4] https://www.visualcapitalist.com/relationship-income-and-wealth/

Chapter 12: Investing: The Life-Changing Power of Opportunity Costs

[1] https://www.financialeducatorscouncil.org

[2] https://www.amazon.com/Messages-Your-Future-Financial-Professional-ebook/dp/B01E4NVUNY

[3] https://www.usfinancialcapability.org/downloads/FINRA_GFLEC_Investor_Knowledge_Report.pdf?utm_source=M-M&utm_medium=email&utm_campaign=S%5FIPC%5F-News%5F103119%5FFINAL

[4] Ibid

[5] https://www.thecalculatorsite.com/finance/calculators/compoundinterestcalculator.php

[6] https://www.thecalculatorsite.com/finance/calculators/carloancalculator.php

Chapter 13: Investing: Time Value of Money and Compounding Interest

[1] https://www.creditcards.com

[2] https://www.creditcards.com/credit-card-news/debt-forever.php

[3] https://www.thecalculatorsite.com/finance/calculators/compoundinterestcalculator.php

[4] http://www.thepeoplehistory.com/70scars.html

[5] http://www.inthe90s.com/prices.shtml

[6] http://www.in2013dollars.com/New-cars/price-inflation

[7] https://www.marketwatch.com/press-release/average-new-car-prices-rise-2-percent-year-over-year-according-to-kelley-blue-book-2018-10-02

[8] https://www.bls.gov/cpi/

Chapter 14: Investing: Investment Vehicles
1 https://www.irs.gov/retirement-plans/401k-plans
2 Ibid

Chapter 15: Investing: Fees and Indexed Mutual Funds
1 https://financiallysimple.com/24-interesting-investing-statistics-you-must-know/
2 https://www.sec.gov/investor/alerts/ib_fees_expenses.pdf
3 https://www.sec.gov

Chapter 16: Investing Risk
1 https://www.investopedia.com/articles/personal-finance/061815/risks-investing-art-and-collectibles.asp
2 https://www.investor.gov/introduction-investing/basics/what-risk
3 https://www.investopedia.com/terms/v/volatility.asp

Chapter 17: Investing: The Short Term Direction Of The Stock Market
1 https://time.com/4777959/buttonwood-agreement-stock-exchange/
2 https://www.cannonfinancial.com/uploads/main/History_of_Investment_Management.pdf
3 Ibid
4 https://business.financialpost.com/investing/investing-pro/beware-of-risk-drag-and-other-tips-for-assessing-your-portfolios-performance
5 https://www.thebalance.com/index-funds-and-efficient-markets-2466394
6 https://www.cnbc.com/2019/01/16/bogle-changed-investing-with-index-funds-but-wasnt-always-happy-about-it.html

7 https://www.cnbc.com/2014/08/19/why-robert-shiller-is-dead-wrong-analyst.html

Chapter 18: Efficient Market Theory Supports Index Funds
1 https://www.econlib.org/library/Enc/bios/Fama.html
2 https://www.investopedia.com/terms/i/indexfund.asp
3 https://www.investopedia.com/terms/d/djia.asp
4 https://www.investopedia.com/ask/answers/12/beating-the-market.asp
5 https://www.aei.org/carpe-diem/more-evidence-that-its-very-hard-to-beat-the-market-over-time-95-of-financial-professionals-cant-do-it/
6 https://www.cnbc.com/2019/03/15/active-fund-managers-trail-the-sp-500-for-the-ninth-year-in-a-row-in-triumph-for-indexing.html
7 https://www.visualcapitalist.com/algorithms-changing-wall-street/
8 https://www.cov.com/en/news-and-insights/insights/2018/11/sec-enforcement-activity-in-2018

Chapter 19: Investing: Build A Diverse Portfolio To Increase Profit And Decrease Risk
1 https://www.investopedia.com/terms/m/modernportfolio-theory.asp
2 https://www.meta-chart.com/pie
3 https://www.marketwatch.com/story/target-date-funds-are-hazardous-to-your-wealth-experts-say-2019-02-20

Chapter 20: Investing: Business Cycles
1 Hallam, Andrew. *Millionaire Teacher, The Nine Rules of Wealth You Should Have Learned in School.* John Wiley & Sons (Asia),

Pte. Ltd. 2011. Page 77.

[2] https://www.bls.gov

[3] https://www.thebalance.com/the-history-of-recessions-in-the-united-states-3306011

Suggested for Further Reading and Study

Messages From Your Future: The Seven Rules for Financial, Personal and Professional Success, by Larry Faulkner

The Index Card: Why Personal Finance Doesn't Have to Be Complicated, by Helaine Olen and Harold Pollack

All Your Worth: The Ultimate Lifetime Money Plan, by Elizabeth Warren and Amelia Warren Tyagi

Personal Finance for Dummies series by Eric Tyson

Asset Allocation for Dummies by Jerry Miccolis and Dorianne Perrucci

Get Rich Slowly blog, getrichslowly.org

The Total Money Makeover, Dave Ramsey

Rich Dad, Poor Dad, by Robert Kiyosaki

The Automatic Millionaire by David Bach

A Random Walk Down Wall Street, by Burton Malkiel

The Bogleheads Guide to Investing, by Taylor Larimore, Mel Lindauer and Michael LeBoeuf

Millionaire Teacher by Andrew Hallam

All About Asset Allocation, by Richard Ferri

Made in the USA
Coppell, TX
29 February 2020